THE CHANGING
TELEVISION AUDIENCE
IN AMERICA

The Changing Television Audience in America

ROBERT T. BOWER

COLUMBIA UNIVERSITY PRESS

NEW YORK   1985

Columbia University Press
New York   Guildford, Surrey
Copyright © 1985 Columbia University Press
All rights reserved

Printed in the United States of America

Library of Congress Cataloging in Publication Data

Bower, Robert T.
    The changing television audience in America.

    Bibliography: p.
    Includes index.
    1. Television audiences—United States—Attitudes—
History.   I. Title.
HE8700.66.U6B68   1985   384.55′44′0973   85-6674
ISBN 0-231-06114-5 (alk. paper)

This book is Smyth-sewn and printed on permanent and durable
acid-free paper.

TO THE MEMORY OF PAUL FELIX LAZARSFELD (1901–1976)
AND HIS BUREAU OF APPLIED SOCIAL RESEARCH (1937–1976)

Contents

Acknowledgments

The work described in this book is a direct descendant of Paul Lazarsfeld and his Bureau of Applied Social Research at Columbia University—pioneers in the study of mass communications audiences. Gary Steiner, the author of the first study in the series, worked at BASR. Frank Stanton, who supported the first two studies, was a colleague of Lazarsfeld's before be became research director and then president of the Columbia Broadcasting System. Joseph Klapper was a student of Lazarsfeld at BASR and the Columbia University graduate school before he went on to run CBS's Office of Social Research, from 1962 until his death in 1984. All three studies in the series received both financial and professional support from Klapper and his excellent staff. I am primarily indebted to that tradition and to those individuals.

Ira Cisin, the consummate social statistician, worked with me on the last two studies. He designed the samples, organized the multivariate analyses, and kept the interpretation of data within proper probability limits. He was an indispensable collaborator in the effort.

The Columbia University Press provided two anonymous scholars to read the manuscript. I have profited greatly from their comments. Wherever you are, many thanks.

Robert T. Bower

THE CHANGING
TELEVISION AUDIENCE
IN AMERICA

CHAPTER ONE

Introduction:
From a Study to a Series

This book reports on a longitudinal series of studies that began with Gary Steiner's 1960 survey, published as *The People Look at Television* (1963). As that title suggests, Steiner's main concern was with the audience of the medium—with the "whom" in the old paradigm of communication research: "who says what to whom through what channel with what effect." Television ownership and control, and the content its producers provided, were pretty much taken for granted. Effect came into the picture only to the extent that audience attitudes might serve to enhance or limit the impact of the medium on its viewers. In his attention to the audience, Steiner was not even particularly interested in how many people watched how much; the final word on that question he was happy to leave to the rating services, who were already operating at full force in 1960. Steiner was interested in what the audience—as a whole and in its various constituent parts—thought about television in general: what in particular they liked and disliked about it; how important they felt it to be; and how it fitted into their lives. He says in his introduction:

> If this book speaks for anyone, we would like to think that it speaks for the audience(s)—not on behalf of, but in echo to. To the extent that we have measured what we set out to measure, these pages should reflect the point of view of the viewer. It is his responses that constitute the data.

Setting the Stage

Steiner designed his study in the late fifties at Columbia University's Bureau of Applied Social Research (BASR), at a time when the Bureau had already experienced two productive decades of audience research under the direction of Paul F. Lazarsfeld. Lazarsfeld had started the Office of Radio Research at Princeton University in 1937 and shortly thereafter had transferred it to Columbia, where it was soon to change its name to the Bureau of Applied Social Research. Between 1940 and Steiner's arrival, Lazarsfeld and his colleagues had published communications research results in more than a dozen major volumes, from Lazarsfeld's *Radio and the Printed Page* in 1940 to *The Effects of Mass Communications* by Joseph Klapper in 1960 (See Barton 1984).

During these years, several of the conceptions about the nature of the audiences' reactions to the mass media that were to guide much communication research in the future were developed. Early on came the idea that some media content might serve to "gratify" psychological needs of audience members. For example, Herta Herzog, in her studies of the audiences of quiz shows (in Lazarsfeld 1940) and of radio soap operas (in Lazarsfeld and Stanton 1944), found that people tended to react favorably because of the personally useful knowledge they thought such programs could provide. The work in this area was the precursor of the now well-established approach to audience research variously termed "needs and gratifications" and "uses and gratifications" (e.g., Blumler and Katz 1974). Other conceptions were developed as ways to help explain the findings of researchers that the mass media had not quite met early expectations about their direct and encompassing effects on the audience. Apparently something was intervening between the media messages and how they were received and acted upon.

The BASR study of the role of the mass media in the 1940 presidential election pointed to the importance of predispositions in determining what people will pay attention to in the media ("selective attention") and how they will interpret it ("selective perception"). This and other work also developed the theory that mass media messages tended to "reinforce" already established personal predispositions, rather than "convert" people from one point-of-view to another (Lazarsfeld, Berelson, and Gaudet 1968; Klapper 1960). A bit later, the idea of "influentials" or "opinion leaders," who acted as conduits between the media and the general public, appeared, leading to the theory of a "two-step-flow" of mass media influence (Merton, in Lazarsfeld & Stanton 1949; Katz & Lazarsfeld 1955).

All this time work was going on at BASR that contributed to the methodology of communication audience research—the Lazarsfeld-Stanton "Program Analyser" to measure immediate reactions to program elements (Lazarsfeld and Stanton 1944); the uses of "deviant case analysis" (Kendall and Wolf in Lazarsfeld and Stanton 1949); the procedures of the "focussed interview" (Merton and Kendall 1946); ways of analyzing the content of communications to which the public was responding (Berelson, 1952); problems of "interviewer bias" (e.g., Udow & Ross, in Lazarsfeld and Stanton 1944). But in research methods as in conceptual developments, BASR was not working alone. Other academic groups, such as the National Opinion Research Center, which started at the University of Denver and then switched to the University of Chicago and Michigan's Survey Research Center, as well as the commercial research organizations run by George Gallup, Elmo Roper, and Archibold Crossley were testing the new waters of cross-sectional sample surveys and perfecting the procedures of personal interviews.

To this research environment, Steiner brought his own orientation as a Chicago-trained psychologist. He was particularly interested in the psychological concept of *projection* and its incorporation into attitude research. Building on other attempts to adapt projective tests to attitude surveys, for instance, he designed for the new study an adaptation of the Thematic Apperception Test in which respondents were asked to react to pictures showing people in a bar, or playing golf, or watching TV, or reading, or just sitting around and chatting. The respondent was asked to say what the people depicted in the little scenes were thinking: "This is really interesting," "I wish I could give this up," "This really does you good," "Boy, this is fun," "What a waste of time." He also made extensive use of questions phrased for the "generalized other" into whose mind the respondent might project his own feelings. For some topics half the sample was asked "how do *you* feel about this?" and the other half was asked "how do *most people* feel about this?" The theory is that people may be willing to project into others the thoughts they would deny for themselves and by comparing the split sample's answers one can discover basic conflicts in the public mind.

Steiner could draw on rather well-developed methodological techniques in the design of the 1960 study. His study employed a form of "modified" probability sampling that permitted the use of quotas to choose respondents after the households had been selected by strict area probability methods—a procedure that had been previously tested by the National Opinion Research Center (NORC). He also employed *two* survey organizations, NORC and Roper, to conduct the interviews, using identical samples of about 1400 cases each. In line with a BASR tradition, the study would add a methodological adjunct to the pursuit of substantive findings— in this case a test of organizationally related interviewer bias. The results were negative, showing no differences at all between the results produced by the two survey groups. The questionnaire contained over 300 items and the interviews lasted up to two hours. In addition, Steiner conducted interviews with a subsample in New York City who had filled out television viewing diaries for the American Research Bureau rating service, so that he could compare what people said about television with what they actually watched.

The first followup study, conducted ten years later at the Bureau of Social Science Research, was not nearly so elaborate. One probability sample of 1900 cases was used and one organization (Roper) conducted the interviewing. The interview lasted about an hour. But despite reduction in scope, every effort was made to replicate what was adopted from the Steiner study as faithfully as possible. We used the same introduction to the study and followed the same sequence of questions throughout the interviewing, adding some new questions at the end. Questions from the 1960 survey were selected for replication in 1970 largely on the basis of their general usefulness in illuminating or interpreting the public's attitudes toward television and in tracing changes in these attitudes over ten years; but there was also concern that the meaning of the responses be unambiguous. We eliminated questions when the terminology seemed shaky (perhaps because the meaning of some words or phrases had changed) or when the system of classifying the answers into code categories was obscure. About half of the

1960 questions were repeated in 1970. To these were added several questions on television's expanding role as a provider of news, questions on educational television, and questions to help interpret the changes that had taken place in the medium over ten years.

The 1980 survey retained most of what had been adopted or added in 1970, with revisions of time-bound questions and a few additions to cover cable television and other developments. The field interviews were again carried out by The Roper Organization using the probability sampling procedure that is described in Appendix A. Some age groups that would have been too thin in numbers for analysis were oversampled. In all, we ended up with over 2000 completed interviews. As in 1970 the exact wording of reused questions was repeated, as was the sequence in which they were asked in the interview, but we did deviate from the past in one respect. In 1960 and 1970, one-city subsamples of American Research Bureau's TV diarists were used for comparisons of attitudes with viewing habits. In 1980 we devised a new method. All respondents were asked what they had done between 7 and 11 o'clock on the evening before the interview. A record was made of everything watched on television. The "last night" diary was used for the comparisons. The procedure limits the detailed analysis of viewing to the prime time hours, but it does permit the use of the entire sample for analysis rather than just a one-city subsample.

Steiner found a 1960 television audience very well disposed toward the medium, primarily for the entertainment it provided. There were many enthusiasts and few critics, the latter mainly among the better-educated viewers. The average viewer, he tells us, "rarely uses the set as a deliberate source of information, and he is extremely unlikely to turn on serious and informative public affairs presentations, even if he is watching while they are on the air." Steiner continues:

All of this reflects the present division of labor among the various media. Television, among the home sources of mass communication, has its greatest comparative advantage in the field of entertainment. According to the average viewer, and no doubt in reality, newspapers presently provide more thorough reports of the important happenings on the local and large scene; radio is quicker with frequent, capsule summaries; and magazines best provide for limited, specialized interests. It is television, and by a wide margin, that is turned to for relaxation and diversion.

That is what changed most between 1960 and 1970—the view of television as almost exclusively an entertainment medium. The second survey showed that television was providing most of the world news the public received, and was starting to be used, rather heavily, as an information medium. The 1970 survey also turned up fewer out-and-out enthusiasts; there was a general overall decline in attitudes toward the medium. In most other respects, the 1970 survey confirmed what had been discovered in 1960: Parents tended to think that television was good rather than bad for their children; the amount of viewing and choice of programs seemed rather unrelated to people's attitude toward the medium; and the main variable separating fans from critics was the respondent's amount of formal education. As the attitudes changed, so did the medium to which people were responding—and so, indeed, did the demographic composition of the public itself.

Growth of Television

Commercial television was of course already well established at the time of the first survey. The networks were in place, most people had sets, and average viewing was up to nearly four hours a day. But there was still room for advancement, as can be seen in table 1.1.

UHF DEVELOPMENT

In 1962 Congress adopted a law permitting the FCC to require that all television receivers be made to receive Ultra High Frequency (UHF) as well as Very High Frequency (VHF) channels. By 1964, this law had given a substantial boost to UHF expansion, and by 1980 the number of UHF stations in operation had tripled. This is of particular significance because many public television

Table 1.1 Changes in the Industry

	Number of Stations and Systems in Operation		
	1960	*1970*	*1980*
Commercial TV			
UHF	75	183	218
VHF	440	508	516
Public TV			
UHF	10	106	168
VHF	34	78	104
CATV Systems	640	2350	4225
	Television Household Data		
Number of sets in use	53 million	88 million	160 million
Percent of all households with TV	87.5	95.5	98
Percent of all household with color TV	a	40	83
Percent of TV households with two or more sets	12.5	30.5	50
Percent of TV sets equipped for UHF	8	52	95
Percent of households with cable TV	a	7.5	23
Channels available to the average household	5 (1964)	7 (1972)	10 (1981)

[a]Less than one percent.
SOURCES: United States Census; Dimension of Television, 1970: Television Factbook, 1970–1980; 1970 and 1980 BSSR survey findings; Nielsen data; Television Almanac, 1981; NAB "Profile: Broadcasting," 1981.

stations were operating on UHF channels which, until the change, had been unavailable to most viewers; the new law served to expand the nature of the programming available to the public.

CABLE TV

In 1949–50, cable TV began to provide a means by which to bring television service to communities outside the reach of broadcast signals. Cable then spread to communities that had television service but who wanted to receive a greater number of stations, or to receive existing stations with greater clarity. In 1950, cable there was available to 14,000 subscribers in seventy communities; by 1980, there were 4225 systems serving more than 16 million subscribers in approximately 10,000 communities. With their larger channel capacities, cable systems are able to offer a wide variety of services: weather and stock market reports, wire service news, uncut and uninterrupted movies, and numerous local programs. At the time of our 1980 survey two-way (interactive) communications through cable, such as the Warner-Amex QUBE System, were in the development stage in many areas of the county.

BROADCAST BY SATELLITE

In 1962, the first live trans-Atlantic telecast by satellite was relayed by Telstar 1; the picture was the American flag fluttering in front of the sending station at Andover, Maine. By 1979, approximately 2000 cable operators owned "earth stations" receiving signals from satellites. Many small satellite networks began to appear to help fulfill cable's promise as an alternative source of diverse specialized programs on an international scale (see Pool 1984).

THE HOME VIDEO MARKET

Home video is electronic equipment enabling the consumer to record and play back sound and images on a standard TV set. These devices can give the consumer direct control not only over what is to be watched, but when. Available in the U.S. consumer electronics market since 1975, the first two months of 1980 saw a 70 percent increase in sales over the same period in 1979; but still they had found their way into only a tiny proportion of the households. The market has since expanded considerably.

Demographic Changes

During the twenty years of the research the distribution of age groups in the adult population has not changed dramatically, and some of the other shifts are quite small (table 1.2). There is a slightly higher proportion of females than in 1960, some increase in the proportion of blacks, a continuation of the shift to cities and suburbs and in the increase of white-collar workers at the expense of their blue-collar counterparts. By far the most significant change has been the spread of education. The proportion of the U.S. adult

Table 1.2 Population Profile, 1960–1980 (In Percentages)

	1960		*1970*		*1980*	
AGE (Base: Persons Aged 18 and Over)						
18–19 years	4.2	} 23.2	5.6	} 28.0	6.0	} 31.0
20–29 years	19.0		22.4		25.0	
30–39 years	21.2	} 40.7	16.9	} 35.0	19.3	} 33.2
40–49 years	19.5		18.9		13.9	
50–59 years	15.6	} 36.0	15.8	} 37.1	14.3	} 36.0
60–64 years	6.1		6.4		6.1	
65 and over	14.3		14.9		15.6	
YEARS OF EDUCATION (Base: Persons 25 and Over)						
Less than High School Graduate	56.5		40.1		33.7	
High School Graduate	26.7		35.7		34.4	
Some College	16.8		24.2		31.9	
SEX (Base: Persons Aged 18 and Over)						
Males	48.3		47.5		46.8	
Females	51.7		52.5		53.5	
RACE (Base: Persons Aged 18 and Over)						
White	89.8		88.9		87.8	
Black	9.4		9.8		10.5	
Other	0.8		1.3		1.5	
OCCUPATION	(Base: Persons 14 and Over)				(Base: Persons 16 and Over)	
White collar	43.1		48.6		53.0	
Blue collar	56.9		51.4		46.9	
GEOGRAPHICAL DISTRIBUTION						
Urban	69.9		73.5		73.9	
Rural	30.1		26.5		26.0	

SOURCE: United States Census.

population without a high school diploma was cut nearly in half between 1960 and 1980, and the proportion of those with some college education almost doubled. Given the high negative correlation between formal education and attitudes toward television, which was found in all three of our surveys, it seems clear that the increased education in the population at large may be an important factor in any overall changes in attitudes toward the medium.

These are only a few of the actual changes that might

have borne some relationship to attitude changes over the past twenty years. Of course the TV programs have changed—no single entertainment series of 1960 has survived into the 1980s—and there were some general trends in the types of programs offered. As news and information programming, for example, more than doubled its proportion of total TV fare, the stimuli to which our samples were responding did not maintain their original shape. Nor has the social and political world stood still. Wars and Watergate, political assassinations and space explorations, and all the other tumultuous events of the past two decades may well have affected how people thought about the medium that brought them the news.

In the following chapters we will be looking at the changes in the public's views about television with such factors in mind. Some of the trends to be examined carry over all three surveys, based upon questions that were developed in 1960 and replicated twice. In other cases, especially in respect to television as a news medium, 1970 becomes the base year for measurement of change, and with even newer developments, such as the use of cable, the data come exclusively from the last of the studies. I have provided with most of the tables and charts to be found in the text the exact wording of the questions asked. Where this has not proved possible, as in the case of multivariable presentations, the reader is referred to Appendix B, where the complete 1980 questionnaire is reproduced. Appendix C contains a discussion of the significance of difference among the percentages found in the text and tables—between and within samples—as a general guide to the reader when differences among subgroups are at issue. For the total samples, differences of 4 percent are significant at the 95 percent level, or 3 percent for percentages around 80 or 20.

CHAPTER TWO

Major Trends

The year 1960 may have been at about the zenith of the public's admiration for television. By this time, the medium that had expanded so rapidly in the preceding ten years was attracting the attention of viewers for an average of four hours a day. For many, there might still have been an aura of novelty surrounding it. In summarizing the findings of his survey, Steiner found that television had already become an integral part of people's daily lives and concluded, conservatively, that the average viewer "feels generally good about television" and that he generally enjoys the programs he watches. He also found that the public turns to the TV set primarily for entertainment and relaxation rather than for information or intellectual stimulation. We will trace here the evolution of these tendencies over the twenty years to 1980, relying on several of the questions in Steiner's survey that were replicated in the two followup studies.

But since the medium itself altered during those twenty years, it would be well to start our discussion of attitudinal trends with a glance at some of the changes in TV content to which the survey respondents were reacting. In 1960 Steiner developed a scheme to classify the programs appearing on television and counted the hours devoted to the different types of programming in one city, New York, during several weeks of the winter of 1959–1960. Seven channels were broadcasting in New York at the time. We used the same scheme in 1970 and 1980 for programs broadcast in both New York and Minneapolis/St. Paul, by stations that could be received in most households. The "Twin Cities" were added to broaden the coverage and because the programs there appeared fairly representative of those offered to the viewers nationally. In both years, two weeks in February were chosen for a count of the programming hours devoted to each of Steiner's categories. In table 2.1, the results for the three studies are given in unduplicated minutes of programming—if programs of the same category appeared on more than one channel simultaneously, that category

Table 2.1 Distribution of Unduplicated Minutes of Television Programming
(In Percentages)

	1960	1970	1980
Light Entertainment	82	72	66
Comedy/Variety (1980 examples are Love Boat, Laverne & Shirley, Taxi)	(22)	(21)	(19)
Movies (except a few classics included under "Heavy Drama")	(20)	(18)	(14)
Action (Barnaby Jones, Fantasy Island, Maverick)	(18)	(16)	(13)
Sports (including rodeo & physical fitness programs)	(9)	(9)	(11)
Light Music (Lawrence Welk, Soul Train)	(4)	(5)	(3)
Light Drama (Dallas, Lou Grant)	(9)	(3)	(6)
News & Information	13	24	27
Regular News (including local news)	(5)	(10)	(8)
Information & Public Affairs (news specials, 60 Minutes, most talk shows)	(8)	(14)	(19)
Heavy Drama (Shakespeare, Moliere, classical movies)	4	2	3
Religion (Billy Graham Crusade, Rex Humbard)	2	3	2
Classical Music	0[a]	0[a]	1
Base: 100 percent =	(2427)	(1900)	(2078)

[a] Less than 0.5 percent.

was counted only once. Thus this method produces low figures for, say, early evening news or Sunday afternoon sports; and it in no way reflects the variety of choices available to the public within categories. It does, however, provide a crude estimate of the proportional attention paid by the broadcasting stations to various kinds of fare.

Table 2.1 shows us that there has been a considerable decrease in the proportion of broadcasting time spent on programs in the "light entertainment" categories. In 1960 light entertainment accounted for about 82 percent of the total fare available to the viewers; by 1980 it was down to 66 percent. News and public affairs programming doubled during the same period—from 13 to 27 percent of the total. These changes in content could well be seen as television's response to the sorts of attitudes expressed by the public in Steiner's study and in the 1970 replication. In both cases the better-educated respondents told the interviewers that they wanted television to do more in providing "informational material" when offered a choice between that and entertainment fare. As we have seen in the summary demographic data of the introductory chapter, that better-educated population has been on the increase during the past twenty years in the United States. The proportion of the population with at least some college education has gone from 17 percent to 32 percent, so some of the content shifts may themselves be reactions to gradual changes in the audience television seeks to serve. The other quantitative change in content that should be noted here is an increase in the number of choices among programs available to the viewers. The addition of more broadcasting stations, the rapid growth of public television, and the production of better receivers and antennae have all added to what could be seen by the average viewer. In addition, cable television has expanded, in the cities surveyed and throughout the country, further increasing the range of program choices available.

Qualitative changes, however difficult to measure, could be even more important. During the past two decades, the white male hegemony in news and public affairs broadcasting has given ground to the incursion of women and blacks, and news cameras have shown viewers dramatic national and international events. News coverage has grown a new, on-the-spot, explicitness, from the shooting of Lee Harvey Oswald to an angry young black hurling a rock at a cop. A similar explicitness has grown in the much larger entertainment portion of broadcasting. There is open treatment of what once would have been shocking: homosexuality, extra-marital affairs, and the like. Arthur Hough (in Adler 1981), who subjected the plots and characters of some 400 situation comedies shown between 1948 and 1978 to a computer-based analysis, concludes that:

> Sitcoms in the last 30 years haven't stood still. they have evolved-from the single, quasi-vaudevillian plots and traditional families of the 1950s, through the upper-middle class nuclear families, the eccentric and fantasy families, and the military and rural themes of the 1960s and then into the social sitcom of the 1970s, with its single parents, working wives, controversial social issues, emancipated women, ethnic plots, sexual issues, and reaffirmation of the work ethic.

Preliminary Questions

Against this background we can now examine the findings of 1980 as they compare with the previous two surveys, following the sequence of questions asked in the same order in each round. As the questioning got underway, the interviewers were careful not to talk about television or indicate that the study would eventually concentrate on that medium. The respondents were told at first only that we were conducting a study "to find out how people feel about various things," and that the answers would be held in confidence. This rather ambiguous introduction permitted an unbiased comparison of television with other things in the series of questions that opened the interview. The first question asked people to say which of several different sorts of things they would choose to keep, if they could have only one. The results of this question (first and second choices) are shown in table 2.2 for each of the three surveys. We see first that television, in each year, comes in no better than fourth after the refrigerator, the car, and the telephone, as something that people feel they must keep in their two- or three-month survival kit. Even though people generally spend more time watching television than doing anything else except sleeping and working, only 5 percent choose television as the one thing they can't do

Table 2.2
"Here are some things that many people take for granted today. But imagine, if you can, that for two or three months you could have only one of these and you'd have to do without the rest."
"If you could only have one of those things, which one would you choose? What would be the second item you'd want?"

	1st Choice			2nd Choice		
	1960	1970	1980	1960	1970	1980
PERCENT WHO SAY:						
Refrigerator	38	38	40	24	31	28
Automobile	31	41	39	28	28	28
Newspaper	11	5	4	12	8	5
Telephone	10	11	11	21	22	24
Television	5	5	5	14	11	14
Don't know, NA	5	1	1	1	0	1
Base: 100 percent =	(2427)	(1900)	(2078)	(2427)	(1900)	(2078)

without. Many more need cars to get to work, refrigerators to keep the dinner from spoiling, and telephones to keep tabs on friends and relatives. The other interesting feature of these results, in a study designed to measure trends in attitudes toward television, is their stability. Over two decades, the proportion choosing television as the one thing they could not do without remains constant at 5 percent and only in the third of the surveys does television change its position, ever so slightly, in comparison with one of the other choices, newspapers. Later in this report, we shall see some fairly dramatic changes in popular views about television; and it is always tempting to emphasize change over consistency. But sometimes changes that might have been expected do not occur, and we shall report that too.

The second question in each of the three surveys asked for relative satisfaction with several consumer "products and services designed to please the general public." As can be seen in table 2.3, television held its position of second place behind automobiles between 1970 and 1980 after a sharp decline in satisfaction during the previous decade. Popular music and movies doubled their proportion of satisfied customers during the seventies but still remained far behind automobiles and TV. A high proportion in 1980 were sufficiently dissatisfied with all the things offered to be unable to choose any of them. The "none" or "don't know" category in-

Table 2.3
"Here is another list of five different products and services designed to please the general public."
"With which of these five things are you personally most satisfied; your second choice?"

	1st Choice			2nd Choice		
	1960	1970	1980	1960	1970	1980
PERCENT WHO SAY:						
Automobiles	48	50	32	24	19	16
Television programs	29	16	16	36	32	20
Fashions for women	11	15	15	13	17	15
Popular music	7	7	14	11	14	11
Movies	2	3	6	8	6	10
None, NA and DK	3	8	17	8	11	28
Base: 100 percent =	(2427)	(1900)	(2078)	(2427)	(1900)	(2078)

creased from 3 percent to 8 percent to 17 percent over the three surveys.

Media Comparisons

The third question in the series, again presented in faithful replication of its first appearance in the Steiner study, consisted of comparisons among four mass media (television, radio, newspapers, and magazines) along 13 different dimensions, as shown in table 2.4. Here we can see some trends in popular attitudes starting to emerge from the data. On the negative side, in 1970 and again in 1980, television is increasingly seen as the medium that "seems to be getting worse all the time," with a corresponding reduction of those choosing it as the one that is getting "better all the time." Television also picks up a few more votes in 1980 as the medium that is "least important to you." It would appear that in some respects the admiration for television in comparison with other media, though still high, is on a downward track.

    At the same time, other items in this question show an opposite trend. The greatest movement in either direction between 1960 and 1970 was on the questions of which of the media "gives the most complete news coverage" (television up 22 percent) and "brings the latest news most quickly" (television up 18 percent). The television vote on both of these items increased again in 1980 by another 10 percent, the largest change recorded. Note too that television increases its votes as the medium that "does the most for the public," which may again indicate a popular shift toward TV journalism while the medium may be losing a bit of the high regard people have had for it in other respects, at least in comparison with radio, newspapers, and magazines. These would appear to be inconsistent, if not contradictory trends, but only if one assumed that the public must see television only *en bloc* and is unable to distinguish among functions the medium may perform. In fact, television serves a variety of purposes and is used in a variety of ways by individual viewers, and the public itself consists of groups of viewers

Table 2.4

"Now, I would like to get your opinions about how radio, newspapers, television, and magazines compare. Generally speaking, which of these would you say. . . ?"

(In Percentages)

Which of the Media:	Television			Magazines			Newspapers			Radio			None/NA		
	1960	1970	1980	1960	1970	1980	1960	1970	1980	1960	1970	1980	1960	1970	1980
Is the most entertaining?	68	72	70	9	5	8	13	9	5	9	14	16	1	0	1
Gives the most complete news coverage?	19	41	51	3	4	5	59	39	33	18	14	10	1	2	1
Presents things most intelligently?	27	38	44	27	18	19	33	28	26	8	9	6	5	8	6
Is the most educational?	32	46	49	31	20	22	31	26	22	3	4	2	3	5	5
Brings you the latest news most quickly?	36	54	64	0	0	1	5	6	5	57	39	30	2	1	1
Does the most for the public?	34	48	51	3	2	2	44	28	26	11	13	13	8	10	8
Seems to be getting worse all the time?	24	41	50	17	18	13	10	14	13	14	5	6	35	22	18
Presents the fairest, most unbiased news?	29	33	36	9	9	9	31	23	20	22	19	18	9	16	16
Is the least important to you?	15	13	17	49	53	46	7	9	13	15	20	19	7	5	5
Creates the most interest in new things going on?	56	61	59	18	16	17	18	14	13	4	5	7	4	5	5
Does the least for the public?	13	10	17	47	50	44	5	7	8	12	13	13	23	20	19
Seems to be getting better all the time?	49	38	31	11	8	12	11	11	10	10	15	21	19	28	24
Gives you the clearest understanding of the candidates and issues in national elections?	42	59	56	10	8	11	36	21	21	5	3	3	7	9	10

1960 Base: 100% = 1900; 1970 Base: 100% = 2427; 1980 Base: 100% = 2078.

that lean in different directions. We shall see more such "inconsist-encies" in later chapters.

Views About Television

At this point, the interviewers explained that the study was really about television—in case the respondents hadn't guessed. Then they introduced a series of questions designed to measure broad, general evaluations of the medium. For this purpose Steiner used the semantic differential technique, adapted from the work of psychologist Charles Osgood (Osgood 1957). Respondents were of-fered a series of contrasting adjectives—interesting–uninteresting, important–unimportant, relaxing–upsetting, and so forth—and asked to choose some position between the two that represented their views of where television stood. Was television *very* interesting, was it *very* dull or somewhere in between?

In the 1960 survey, which we copied for 1970 and 1980, seventeen opposites were presented, each with six positions in be-tween. The more favorable-seeming adjective was sometimes on the left, sometimes on the right, of the page. The technique was de-signed to get quick, top-of-the-head, reactions, and interviewers were instructed to discourage studious reflection about each adjec-tive. In tables 2.5 and 2.6, the results for the three surveys are presented in two parts. In table 2.5 are the pairs of adjectives that seem quite clearly directional—"relaxing" is more favorable than "upsetting," "interesting" better than "uninteresting," and so forth. The attitudinal direction of those in table 2.6 is less clear.

Table 2.5, with the proportions choosing various of the positions on the scale (middle positions combined), shows the con-tinuation of a trend that was observed in 1970: attitudes toward television, very favorable in 1960, down a bit in 1970, are, by 1980, even more depressed. But note that the decline is from the top, with the average proportions choosing the most favorable position (1) going from 33 percent in 1960 to 19 percent in 1980. Although about two-thirds still remain on the favorable side [(1), (2) and (3)], there appears to be a definite fading of enthusiasm, but one that stops far short of rejection. The least favorable position (6) hardly

Table 2.5

"Here are some opposites. Please read each pair quickly and put a check some place between them, wherever you think it belongs to describe television. Just your offhand impression."

Television is Generally: Proportion of three samples choosing various scale positions

	(1)			(2) & (3)			(4) & (5)			(6)			
	1960	1970	1980	1960	1970	1980	1960	1970	1980	1960	1970	1980	
Relaxing	43	33	24	40	50	45	12	15	27	4	4	4	Upsetting
Interesting	42	31	25	40	47	49	13	18	22	4	5	4	Uninteresting
For me	41	27	23	35	44	44	16	23	24	8	8	8	Not for me
Important	39	30	25	38	43	42	17	22	26	6	7	8	Unimportant
Informative	39	35	28	45	50	56	13	12	12	3	3	4	Not informative
Lots of fun	32	22	18	45	51	47	17	22	25	6	6	7	Not much fun
Exciting	30	19	17	47	52	53	18	24	25	4	7	6	Dull
Wonderful	28	19	12	49	51	52	20	28	31	3	6	4	Terrible
Imaginative	26	19	17	49	53	51	20	22	25	5	7	7	No imagination
In good taste	24	18	14	52	52	48	25	26	31	4	7	8	In bad taste
Generally excellent	22	15	11	51	54	44	23	27	38	5	6	7	Generally bad
Average of Eleven Items	33	24	19	45	50	48	18	22	26	5	6	6	

1960 Base: 100% = 2427; 1970 Base: 100% = 1900; 1980 Base: 100% = 2078.

Table 2.6
Television is Generally:

	Positions (1) & (2)			Positions (3) & (4)			Positions (5) & (6)			
	1960	1970	1980	1960	1970	1980	1960	1970	1980	
Lots of variety	51	48	43	31	35	36	18	17	21	All the same
On everyone's mind	55	39	34	39	49	48	7	12	18	Nobody cares much
Getting better	44	31	22	40	44	40	17	26	38	Getting worse
Keeps changing	40	40	34	40	44	46	19	17	20	Stays the same
Serious	16	15	16	60	52	67	24	17	18	Playful
Too "highbrow"	7	7	6	71	71	66	20	23	28	Too "simple minded"

1960 Base: 100% = 2427; 1970 Base: 100% = 1900; 1980 Base: 100% = 2078.

moves at all. On one of the pairs of adjectives, the public has changed its views very little. In 1960, 84 percent of the sample chose one of the three top positions for television as "informative." Twenty years later that figure was still 84 percent. This would seem in line with the public's continuation of its high regard for television as a news and information medium, as noted above, even when attitudes in general are declining.

Other adjectival pairs, shown in table 2.6, are also worth brief comment. Two of these items show about the same degree of decline in pro-TV attitudes we saw among the items of table 2.5. People are less likely to believe that television is "on everyone's mind," possibly a perceptive change in assessments as the medium has come of age and lost the glamor of novelty, and fewer people think that television is "getting better" (or more think it is "getting worse"), putting in trend form the attitude that is otherwise shown in the three separate readings. On two items that might be considered measures of television's triviality, the public comes down rather squarely in the middle. Most people think television is about halfway between "serious" and "playful" and neither "to highbrow" nor "too simple-minded" but, again, somewhere in between.

These are variations from the central finding of this series of questions—the general decline in enthusiasm for television. In 1970, at the first reading of attitude changes over a decade, it appeared that the trend was not uniform across the population as might have been the case had not so many respondents in 1960 chosen positions at the most favorable extreme that the scale allowed. In 1970 the main change was a decline in the number of these superfans. The ranks of the vilifiers—those on the extreme unfavorable end—changed hardly at all. The major gains came in the middle positions (table 2.7). Between 1970 and 1980, the biggest shift was again away from the very top to somewhere lower in the scale; the average of the percentages in the top of the six positions went from 24 percent to 19 percent, with the gains spread across most of the other positions.

A summary measure of attitudes toward television was developed using choices on seven of the "semantic differential" items (specifically exciting–dull; important–unimportant; generally excellent–generally bad; in good taste–in bad taste; interesting–

Table 2.7 Average of Proportions Choosing Each of Six Positions

	1960	1970	1980	1960–1980 Shifts
Most Favorable (1)	33	24	19	−14
(2)	20	20	18	−2
(3)	25	30	30	+5
(4)	13	16	17	+4
(5)	5	6	9	+4
Least Favorable (6)	5	4	6	+1
Base: 100 percent =	(2427)	(1900)	(2078)	

uninteresting; wonderful–terrible; for me–not for me). Each respondent was given a score from zero for choosing the least favorable position for an item to five for the most favorable among the six points in the scale. When the scores were added for the seven items, summary attitude scores could range from zero for someone who despised television to 35 for the superfan, with the most neutral point resting at 17.5. Using this method of computation, the average attitude scores for the whole population on three surveys were 24.3 in 1960, 22.3 in 1970 and 20.9 in 1980.

With these scores as the dependent variables, all three surveys were subjected to a multivariate analysis, with twelve independent variables interrelated through the "Automatic Interaction Detection" computer program, which sorts out the variables that best explain high and low attitudes. The twelve variables held constant are age, sex, race, family income, education, religion, occupation, presence of children in the household, political party preference, leaning toward liberalism or conservatism, region of the country, and population concentration. The main results of the analyses are shown in figures 2.1, 2.2, and 2.3.

In all three surveys two variables lead all the others in accounting for differences in attitudes toward television when the other variables are held constant. Education appears as the primary variable in 1960, explaining the largest proportion of the variance, with race a close second. In 1970 and 1980 race accounts for the largest proportion of the variance with education in second place. Blacks like television better than do whites, and the less educated like it more than the better educated, each where the effect of eleven

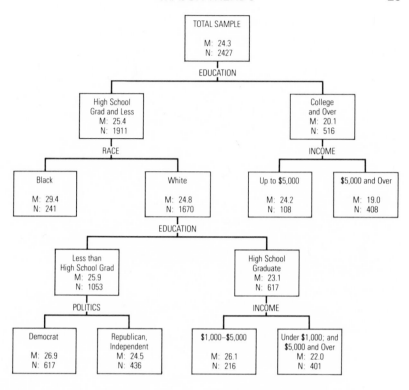

FIGURE 2.1. 1960 Attitude Scores

additional variables is taken into account. None of the other factors survive the analyses with any consistency, though here and there region of the country, party preference, and income make brief appearances. Together, education, race, income, party preference and region accounted for 19.4 percent of the total variance in 1980. Despite the abiding myth that women like TV better than men, there is no evidence in the 1980 study, nor in the two that preceded it, that such is the case.

The persistence of educational levels and race differences as the main variables associated with attitudes toward tele-

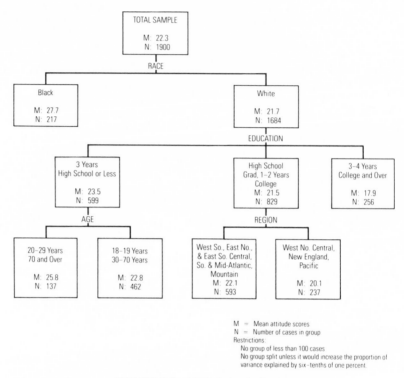

FIGURE 2.2. 1970 Attitude Scores

vision, while attitudes overall were declining, would suggest that education and racial subgroups might have shared differentially in that decline. In table 2.8 we can see the average attitude scores for several subgroups in 1960 and 1980. (The 1970 scores are in all cases somewhere in between.) The decline in general attitudes toward television has been rather uniform across *all* segments of the population. Men and women, close in 1960 in their views about the medium, remained so after twenty years with a few points off their attitude scores. Each age group (especially the teenagers) and both occupational categories shared in the trend.

Blacks, always more friendly to TV than whites, actually increased the disparity between the races by maintaining a bit more of their allegiance, but both groups showed lower scores. The educational subgroups actually show lower declines in attitude scores

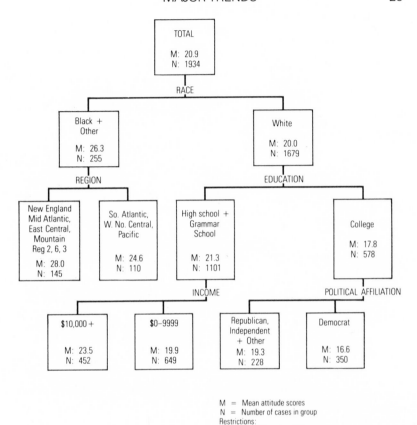

FIGURE 2.3. 1980 Attitude Scores

than the overall average of about 14 percent. With the general rise in education in the United States, there are simply more people in the better educated categories, where attitudes are apt to be lower, than there were twenty years ago. For example, the college-educated proportions in the samples increased from 22 percent in 1960 to 34 percent in 1980. If we were to take the 1960 attitude scores for each of these educational groups and simply adjust the scores on the basis of the 1980 population distribution, we would project a 1980 attitude score of 23.2 for the total sample, a decrease of 1.1 points

Table 2.8 Attitude Scores, 1960 to 1980 by Population Subgroups

	1960	1980	Percent Decrease
SEX			
Male	24.1	20.8	14
Female	24.2	20.8	14
RACE			
White	23.6	19.8	16
Black	28.6	26.3	8
EDUCATION			
Grade school	26.7	25.1	6
High school	24.5	21.5	12
College	20.0	18.1	10
AGE			
18, 19	25.5	20.5	20
20–29	23.0	20.7	10
30–39	23.4	20.1	14
40–49	24.0	19.5	19
50–59	25.0	20.7	17
60+	25.4	22.5	11
OCCUPATION, HEAD OF HOUSEHOLD			
White collar	21.6	17.9	15
Blue collar	25.6	20.9	18
RESPONDENTS IN HOUSEHOLD WITH CHILDREN UNDER 15			
Yes	23.8	20.6	14
No	24.8	20.8	16
PARTY CHOICE			
Democratic	25.1	21.8	13
Republican	23.4	19.7	16
Independent	22.2	18.8	15

(or 4.6 percent) from the 1960 score that could be attributed to the redistribution of education among the population alone. To translate—about a third of the 14 percent attitude decline in the total population has resulted from the increase in education in the United States.

If we had no other data to examine, we might assume that the decline in enthusiasm for the medium would have been associated with a decrease in the amount of time people chose to spend in front of the set, and certainly with a decline in the amount of enjoyment they derived from their viewing. In point of fact, neither of these presumed accompaniments of attitude change took place. During the twenty years, the average amount of viewing increased according to our own data (discussed in the next chapter) and according to the continuous and perhaps more reliable data from the rating services, who report to the industry on audience sizes. The viewing of the average adult American increased at a steady pace up until the mid-1970s, when it seems to have leveled off. In 1980, an average viewer was watching about 20 percent more television than he had watched in 1960. Are viewing and expressed attitudes such unrelated phenomena that they can proceed in opposite directions?

Viewer Satisfaction

The mystery deepens when we examine the possibility that the decline in attitudes may be the result of less personal satisfaction found in the increased viewing. People watching more television (for whatever reason) see more that they don't like, and they express their dissatisfaction through the battery of adjectival descriptions that make up our attitude scale. Fortunately, Steiner included in his survey a question designed to tap people's reactions to the programs they actually watched on television as distinct from their views about the medium in general. We repeated the question in the subsequent surveys, with the results shown in figures 2.4 and 2.5. Figure 2.4 shows the percent in each sample that thought various proportions of the program they watched were "extremely enjoyable." In 1960, 14 percent of the people interviewed thought that more than three quarters of the programs they watched were "extremely enjoyable," a bit more than half the sample thought that between a quarter and three quarters of the programs they watched were "extremely enjoyable," and 32 percent thought only a quarter or less of the programs deserved that description. By 1980, the proportion who thought that most of the programs (76 percent or more) were "extremely enjoyable" had risen to 28 percent and those who thought only a quarter of the programs were "extremely en-

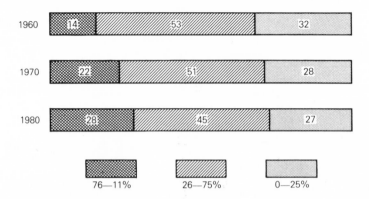

FIGURE 2.4. Proportion of Programs Felt To Be "Extremely Enjoyable."
"Television programs, like most other things, vary in quality. Some are better
than others. Considering just the programs you generally watch, what proportion
would you say are extremely enjoyable, how many are somewhat enjoyable,
how many are just so-so, and how many are disappointing? First, what percentage of the TV programs you watch would you call extremely enjoyable?"

joyable" had dropped to 27 percent. More people were enjoying more
of the program they watched.

Figure 2.5 presents the data separately for each of the
three education groups. The computation is somewhat simplified
to show the average proportions of programs that each subgroup
finds to be "extremely enjoyable." In this figure we see the expected
differences among the education groups, with the better educated
finding a lower proportion of their programs to be "extremely enjoyable" in each year. In 1980 the figures are 60 percent for the
grade schoolers, 55 percent for the high school graduates, and 51
percent for those with some college. These differences are consistent
with the attitudinal differences among the education groups found
elsewhere in the study. The better educated respondents think less
of television in general and enjoy fewer of the programs they watch.
The discrepancy between attitudes and enjoyment over time, however, is again quite striking. All three groups, which we have shown
to be falling off in their general regard for television, are now telling
us that they are enjoying more of what they see.

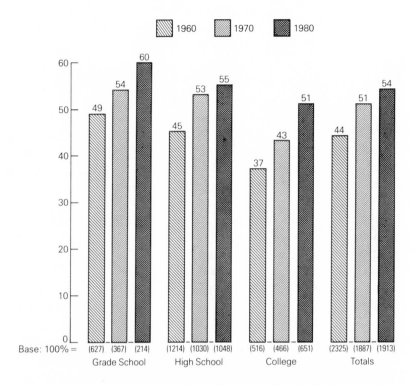

FIGURE 2.5. Average Proportion of Programs Felt To Be "Extremely Enjoyable" (by Education)

The explanation of this apparent contradiction may lie in part in changes in the medium itself. The number of broadcasting stations has increased, cable television has entered a quarter of the households, and sets have been improved so that more channels can be reached. The larger number of programs available to the average viewer at any one time would permit him to be more selective in his choices, indeed permit him to find more programs that he would find "extremely enjoyable" even when it was his impression that the general quality of TV fare was declining.

Added to this, there is the distinct possibility that we are dealing with dimensions of attitudes that need not vary in any concordant pattern. In analyzing his 1960 data, Steiner distinguished among three facets of people's attitudes toward television's content. First, there are views about what sorts of programs *should* be shown, as expressed in answers to questions about desires for more entertainment vs. more informational fare, or the series of questions we shall discuss later in this report on types of programs we should have more of, or less of. Then there are views about the current general content of television, which may be revealed in answers to questions about television in general, such as the semantic differential items which we have just discussed, or many other items in our questionnaire about specific parts of the menu of programs that is offered to the public. And third, there are views about the programs the respondent actually watches; how does he feel about what he himself has chosen to watch? Steiner found that views on these three dimensions often diverged. People with very negative attitudes toward television in general often seemed to enjoy the programs they themselves watched, even when their choices were not so very different from those of the TV fans; and people who said that the networks should offer a certain type of program didn't necessarily watch these programs when they were available. Further, when viewers watched programs of the sort they said they *didn't* like, they tended to see virtues in them which others did not see. Thus, for example, some of the better educated respondents, when talking about programs they had seen in the scorned "light drama," "action," or "comedy-variety" categories, might credit them with an "intellectual" quality more readily than would those whose general attitudes corresponded more closely with their program choices.

This tendency to reduce dissonances by finding the proper qualities in favorite programs could help to explain why expressed attitudes toward the medium and views about one's own chosen programs could proceed on divergent paths for some of the respondents in the surveys. We should note also the possibility that some people may enjoy (or increasingly enjoy) programs of which they don't at all approve. Freudian psychology suggests that such a circumstance generates guilt in Western man, and indeed there is some evidence in the data that an increasing proportion of the public is feeling uncomfortable about the amount of television that is being viewed. The samples were asked in 1960 and in the subsequent surveys the question: "Do you think that you spend too much time watching television or that you don't see as much as you would really like (to see)?" The proportion of those who say they are spending "too much time" has increased from 17 percent of the 1960 sample to 24 percent in 1980.

To summarize the broad trends over the twenty years, the American public appears to have less regard for television as a medium than it did, but it uses television more, especially to keep informed, and it enjoys it more, though it isn't quite sure that it should.

CHAPTER THREE

The Changing Audiences

The amount of television watched by the United States public has been measured continuously by the syndicated rating services, chiefly Nielsen and Arbitron, throughout the entire time period of our studies. Though their high count has been questioned by some communication researchers (e.g., Robinson 1977), they provide a better guide than is found in this series of studies. Our entry into the measurement of audience sizes is primarily for analytic purposes, so that we can relate the amount of viewing to other variables such as the demographic characteristics of the viewers and their attitudes. In the original Steiner study, people were asked to indicate each hour they ordinarily watched some television—in effect to report on their usual patterns of *likely* viewing rather than *actual* viewing. The same procedures were used in 1970 and 1980. In 1980 we added a bit more data on prime-time audience size by asking the respondents what they were doing on the night before the interview, for each half hour between 7 and 11 P.M. In the discussion which follows we draw on both sets of data.

The hour-by-hour patterns of likely viewing on weekdays, Saturday, and Sunday are shown for all three surveys in table 3.1. Between 1960 and 1970 there appeared to be an increase in viewing in almost every time slot, resulting in an overall increase of slightly under 20 percent as measured by this somewhat imprecise method. Nielsen's tallies show an increase of 17 percent for the same period, as shown in the following tallies, in hours and minutes, from Nielsen's reports on total household viewing:

1960;	5:03
1970;	5:56
1980;	6:26

During the next ten years, average viewing increased overall by a much smaller amount—7 percent by our measures, 8 percent according to Nielsen, and the pattern was altered. Most of the increases

Table 3.1

"On an average day; during what hours do you yourself ordinarily watch television?"

(Likely Viewing 1960–1980)

| | Percentage Checking Each Time Period | | | | | | | | |
| | Weekdays | | | Saturday | | | Sunday | | |
Hours	1960	1970	1980	1960	1970	1980	1960	1970	1980
Morning:									
6:00– 7:00	2	4	7	1	2	4	1	2	2
7:00– 8:00	5	8	12	1	4	7	1	3	5
8:00– 9:00	6	8	12	3	7	9	2	7	7
9:00–10:00	8	8	14	5	8	11	4	7	10
10:00–11:00	10	12	14	6	9	12	5	8	12
11:00–12:00	12	15	17	7	10	16	6	10	13
Afternoon:									
12:00– 1:00	14	21	22	8	14	17	9	15	17
1:00– 2:00	12	18	21	13	17	19	14	21	25
2:00– 3:00	13	19	20	15	21	21	19	26	28
3:00– 4:00	11	17	18	13	21	22	20	26	27
4:00– 5:00	11	19	19	12	20	21	21	24	24
Early Evening:									
5:00– 6:00	16	31	36	14	24	25	22	25	28
6:00– 7:00	35	55	57	29	40	37	35	39	42
Evening:									
7:00– 8:00	57	63	63	50	53	46	52	56	51
8:00– 9:00	69	69	67	57	60	52	61	65	56
9:00–10:00	66	66	66	56	58	51	58	63	55
10:00–11:00	42	48	55	40	46	44	38	44	43
Late Evening, Early Morning:									
11:00–12:00	15	20	26	20	24	26	14	17	19
12:00– 1:00	7	7	11	9	11	14	6	5	7
1:00– 2:00	2	3	6	3	5	9	2	2	5
2:00– 3:00	1	2	4	1	3	6	1	1	3

Base: 1960 100% = 2427; 1970 100% = 1900; 1980 100% = 2078.

came during the previously ill-attended hours—morning and late night—whereas the prime time hours of seven to eleven remained about the same; and indeed showed some declines. As we noted ten years ago, the prime time audience had by 1970 about reached its limit if we assume that people must spend some time eating dinner, reading a book, taking a nap, seeing a movie, visiting a friend, or working.

There are of course variations in the sheer amount of television watching among subgroups of the population. Some of these differences, uncovered rather consistently in various investigations, are summarized for us by Comstock, et al. (1978) in their comprehensive review of television research. Comstock relies heavily on Nielsen Company reports for his viewing data. We are told the following:

- Women watch more television than men.
- Those of lower socioeconomic status (SES)—the poorer and the less educated—watch more than those of higher SES.
- Blacks watch more than whites.
- People over 50, especially women, watch more than others.
- The fewer the people living in a household, the more the viewing.

The data in our three studies support these general findings when one looks at the amount of "likely" viewing reported by the various subgroups in the population for the weekday and weekend hours, and even when one uses the "last night" diary results. For the *total* sample, the diaries indicated that about 17 percent were not at home at all between 7 and 11 P.M. and thus watched no television, about 39 percent were at home at least part of the time and spent all of that at-home time watching television, and about 14 percent were at home at least part of the time and spent *none* of it watching television. On the average, the sample spent about an hour and a half before the set during the evening, with the differences in allocation by subgroups shown in the first column of table 3.2. In line with the findings quoted above, women watched more than men (to a small degree), the less educated more than the better, the older viewers more than the younger, and blacks more than whites. Contrary to other findings, however, members of households with only one adult reported somewhat less viewing than those in two-adult households. The differences are certainly not large, but they are there—even for the prime-time period.

Some of the differences that do exist among subgroups may in part be explained by the average proportion of time each group spent at home the preceding night during the four-hour

Table 3.2 Television Viewing 7–11 P.M. by Population Subgroups

	Percent of Time Spent Viewing	Percent of Time at Home	Percent of At-Home Time Spent Viewing	(N: Approxi-mate Hrs.)
SEX				
Male	42	70	60	(3250)
Female	45	80	57	(4950)
EDUCATION				
Grade school	49	85	58	(2150)
High school	42	75	59	(3350)
Some college	39	65	58	(2550)
AGE				
18–29	43	71	56	(3100)
30–50	46	76	60	(2300)
51 +	48	81	59	(2200)
RACE				
White	43	76	57	(7200)
Black	47	73	65	(400)
ADULTS IN HOUSEHOLD				
One	42	72	58	(1400)
Two	46	78	58	(4850)
Three or more	43	75	57	(1550)

period (the second column of table 3.2). If we measure viewing only during the time people were at home, we arrive at a figure, for the total sample, of just under three-fifths of the time at home spent watching television, with the variations among groups shown in the third column of table 3.2. Men were out of the house more than women, but when they were at home they actually spent more time watching television. When this at-home measure is used as a basis, the only other differences that appear at all pronounced are between whites and blacks, with the latter viewing more during the smaller amount of time at home. But it would appear that all groups watch roughly similar amounts of television in the evening, if they are at home where the set is.

This analysis would not be complete, however, without a consideration of the separate effects of two variables that are themselves interrelated. With the rapid spread of education in the United States, the younger adults in the population are apt to be better educated than the older; conversely, the less-educated are found disproportionately among the over-50 age group. We can examine the effect of each variable, with the other held constant, by means of a simple three-variable table which gives the proportion of at home time spent watching TV on the previous evening for each age group within each educational group (table 3.3). We see that even in combination age and education make very little difference in the amount of television watched, as long as people are at home.

Another measure of intergroup differences in the amount of time spent viewing may be derived by an analysis of the hours of likely viewing tabulations shown before in table 3.1. For this analysis we adopt the concept of the "equal opportunity" audience, measuring the amount of viewing for those hours when all adults have about an equal chance of watching TV unimpeded by work demands. We assume that most people can be at home and can turn on the set on weekdays after 6:00 P.M. and all day on Saturday and Sunday. The viewing times we have counted in all three surveys to assign amount-of-viewing scores to the respondents are limited to those hours. This goes a long way toward equalizing the opportunity for viewing between women (who are more apt to be at home during the day) and men (who are more apt to be at work), and for that matter, between working and nonworking people of either sex. It may give a fairly equal chance for a working man or woman and a retired person to be recorded as a heavy or light viewer. In this attempt to equalize opportunity, we are using a measure that maximizes the viewing that results from an inclination to turn on the set when the members of the public are not prevented from doing so by the demands of work.

If we equalize the opportunity for viewing in that way

Table 3.3 Proportion of At-Home Time Spent Viewing: 7–11 P.M. by Age and Education

	Age		
	18–29 Yrs.	*30–50 Yrs.*	*Over 50*
Grade school	58	57	58
High school	53	64	59
College	57	59	59

and then subject the data to a multivariate analysis (AID) which incorporates the same thirteen background variables as in the analysis of attitudes in the previous chapter, we emerge with the conclusion that such factors as age, sex, race, and educational level make relatively little difference in how much television is watched (figures 3.1, 3.2, and 3.3). In 1960 none of these factors were significant enough to explain, independently of the others, more than half of one percent of the variance. In 1970 selective ages and family incomes appeared to have some association with viewing when other effects were controlled, but only as secondary factors and in a manner that is not consistent with findings of other research on total viewing. In 1980 education appears to explain a small amount of the variance, at a secondary level. In places of a certain size, the

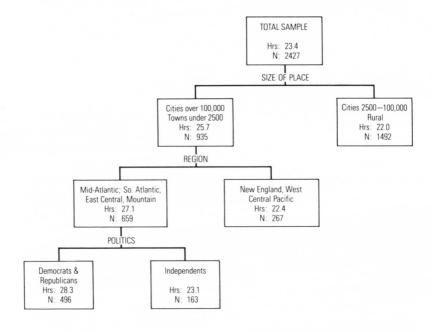

FIGURE 3.1. 1960 Viewing

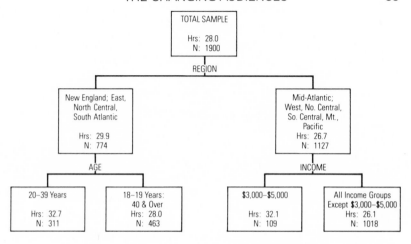

FIGURE 3.2. 1970 Viewing

high school graduates view more than the college-educated and gradeschoolers.

The two factors that appear over the years to have made the most differences in "equal opportunity" viewing are geographic—the population concentration and the region of the country in which people live. Generally people seem to have watched more television if they lived in larger cities, other things being equal. Among the high-viewing regions in the United States there is very little consistency over the twenty-year period. New England, for example, appears among the high-viewing areas in 1970 and 1980 and among the low-viewing areas in 1960. One suspects that if the community's population and its geographic region influence viewing, as they appear to do, it is not because people living in different places are motivated differently. It is much more likely that we are observing differences in opportunity to watch because of the distribution of broadcasting stations and the strength of signals or because of extraneous factors, like weather, that might affect people's perceptions of how much they ordinarily watched television. There

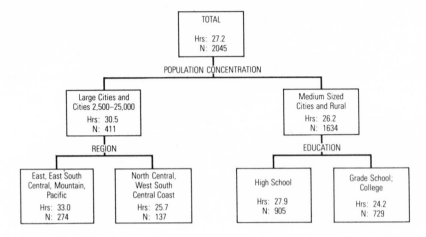

FIGURE 3.3. 1980 Viewing

is also the possibility of a statistical artifact. With a discontinuous variable like geographic area the AID program can find any combinations among the nine census regions (e.g., grouping New England with the West Central) to maximize the statistical difference in a split into groupings of high and low-viewing regions. In any case, it is interesting to note that in 1980 there were only three factors that survived the AID test of explaining at least half of one percent of the variance—size of place, region, and education. In combination these three factors explained only 4.9 percent of the total variance.

Most important, however, is that the analysis does not show that those variables which have traditionally been thought to be most influential have any particular effect on television viewing. If we remove most of the variation that is caused by opportunity and adjust for the interrelated effects of various factors that might have some influence on viewing, we find very little effect left. A person's age sex, race, education, or income make little difference—

everyone views television about the same amount except when prevented from doing so by external factors, like work.

Ages of Viewing

A great deal of television research in the United States has been devoted to young viewers. When still members of the Sesame Street set they learn the basics, and as they get a bit older they absorb antisocial TV content. On the latter score, the Surgeon General's Scientific Advisory Committee on Television and Social Behavior was responsibile for conducting or stimulating many of the more careful studies of the effect of TV on aggression among children during the early 1970s. Comstock and his colleagues (1978) provide a rather complete summary of the findings of research on children in a chapter entitled "One Highly Attracted Public." Our own interest really starts when people reach 18 and become members of an adult sample, but how much—and what—they watched earlier is still relevant: previous viewing habits set patterns and established attitudes toward the medium that persist into adulthood. A decade or so ago, there was a theory abroad concerning a "television generation" whose ideas had been established during their formative years, as they grew up with the new and exciting medium, and these ideas were expected to persist into adulthood. An analog of this theory is found in political behavior, where some political scientists have found a tendency for young people to form political loyalties and preferences that persist as they go on through life (Cutler 1970).

There is of course a contrary conception, held particularly by those of sociological background. It says that people change in the way they act toward, and what they feel about, something like television as a result of the changing circumstances they meet as they go through life—leaving home, getting married, raising children, slowing down. People's social environments and needs change at each stage, which is what affects behavior and attitudes.

These two competing theories were tested in the previous report on the 1960 and 1970 data through a cohort analysis which compared the consistency of opinion within generations (e.g., 18–19-year-olds of 1960 and 28–29-year-olds of 1970). By and large, the stage-of-life theory won out over the generational. As people got older it appeared that they conformed to views about television held by their age group; they seemed not to carry forward the viewws of ten years before. Graphs of the 1960 and 1970 data are shown again in figures 3.4 through 3.7 with the 1980 data added.

The lines in figure 3.4 show, by age groups and for each of the three surveys, the average amounts of weekly viewing during weekday evening and weekend hours. The viewing of 18- and 19-year-olds in 1970 and 1980 is relatively low. This is probably in line with a trend that has been noted elsewhere on children's viewing of television. Comstock (1978) summarizes data to show that the peak viewing age for children (in the 1970s) was about 12, when an average of four hours a day was watched, falling off to about three hours a day at ages 19 and 20. Though our viewing data are not measured in the same fashion and are not exactly comparable, it would seem that our teenagers are in that viewing trough. The teenagers of two decades ago, however, were the most assiduous viewers of all, even edging out the old folks over 60. This high viewing among the 1960 young people could perhaps be a statistical artifact, since only 84 cases were included in the 1960 sample. But we could give the sampling its due and speculate that in 1960 the medium was new enough to capture the venturous attention of young people. If so, it did not similarly engage the people in their twenties that year, and we would have to assume that television had become old hat for teenagers ten years and twenty years later. It's certainly possible.

Pursuing the 1970 and 1980 age groups in figure 3.4 a bit further, we can see the increase in viewing during the 20s, the falling off in the 30s and 40s, the rise in the 50s and the decline again among the over 60s, creating a pattern that is strking in its similarity in two independent samplings ten years apart. The young age groups of 1960, below 30, clearly followed their own pattern, but from age 30 on, they too follow the same viewing lines of the

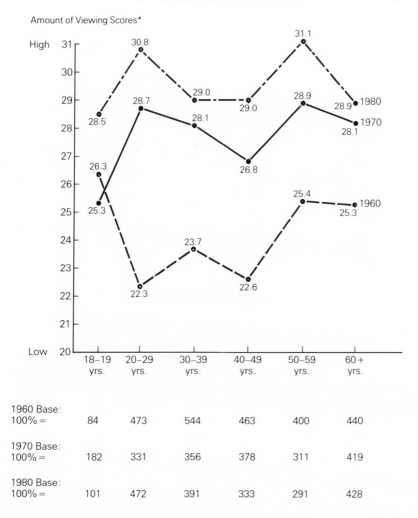

FIGURE 3.4. Amount of Viewing

later decades. At least one thing is consistent—a relatively larger amount of viewing by people in their 50s in all three surveys.

The other graphs show patterns by age with striking similarities among the three surveys. In figure 3.5 is the proportion of each age group that choose television as the thing with which

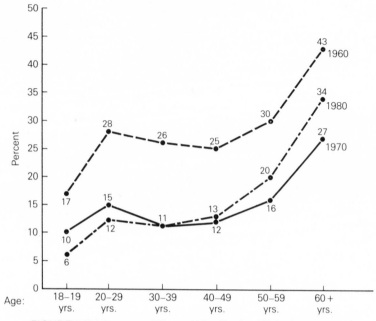

FIGURE 3.5. Percent of Those Who Reply: "Television"
"With which of these five things are you personally most satisfied (cars, TV programs, fashions, popular music, movies)?"

	18–19 yrs.	20–29 yrs.	30–39 yrs.	40–49 yrs.	50–59 yrs.	60+ yrs.
1960 Base: 100% =	84	473	544	463	400	440
1970 Base: 100% =	182	331	356	378	311	419
1980 Base: 100% =	110	487	400	335	295	438

they are "most satisfied," among a list that includes cars, popular music, and movies. The continuing relative appeal of the latter three items for young people, and particularly teenagers, probably explains the shape of the curves, with television becoming relatively more "satisfying" as people get older. The curve for the 1980 sample goes from 6 percent of the teenagers finding television the most satisfactory to 34 percent of those over 60. When comparisons are made from a different list of universally used items, we find a different pattern of responses by age groups, as shown in figure 3.6. For all ages, television ranks fairly low in comparision with refrig-

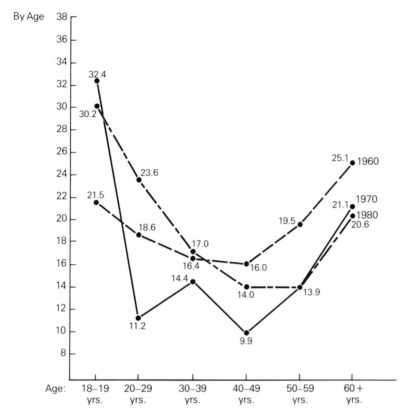

FIGURE 3.6. Percent Who Chose Television (1st and 2nd Choice Combined) "Here are some things that many people take for granted today. But imagine, if you can, that for two or three months you could have only one of these and have to do without the rest. Which one would you choose (refrigerator, car, newspapers, telephone, TV)?"

1960 Base:						
100% =	84	473	544	463	400	440
1970 Base:						
100% =	182	331	356	378	311	419
1980 Base:						
100% =	110	487	400	335	295	438

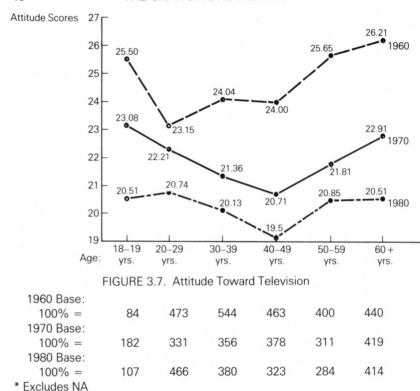

FIGURE 3.7. Attitude Toward Television

	18–19 yrs.	20–29 yrs.	30–39 yrs.	40–49 yrs.	50–59 yrs.	60 + yrs.
1960 Base: 100% =	84	473	544	463	400	440
1970 Base: 100% =	182	331	356	378	311	419
1980 Base: 100% =	107	466	380	323	284	414

* Excludes NA

erators and automobiles as a necessity for existence over a two or three month period, but it ranks lowest during the family-raising middle years, when cars and refrigerators may be particulary important and higher for the teenagers and those 50 and over. Finally, in figure 3.7 the summary attitudes scores—relatively high among the youngest and older age groups and lower in the middle—are plotted.

The patterns shown differ markedly from graph to graph, with each age group sometimes low and sometimes high, depending on the particular attitude question that is plotted; but the shape of each graph has some reasonable explanation related to the stages of life through which the age groups are progressing. Overall, the graphs would tend to confirm once more that attitudes do vary by stages of life with little generational effect discernible.

There is another respect in which age is clearly related to attitudes on television; some types of televison content are far more likely to be applauded by the young than by the old. In 1970 we were able to ask two questions about matters that were being given a good deal of attention in the media:

From your point of view, does television have enough, not enough or too many programs that provide information about social problems in the U.S., like racial problems and problems on the college campuses?

As far as your own viewing is concerned, is more live coverage of disruptions in the U.S. such as riots and protests in the streets a change for the better, a change for the worse or hasn't it made any difference to you?

During the late sixties the civil rights protest movement was at its height (Martin Luther King was assassinated in 1968) and so was the anti-Vietnam war protest. "Moratorium Day" occurred in 1969. With such events as the referents for the questions, the public divided quite sharply along age lines, with 45 percent of those over 60 saying there were too many programs about "social problems and problems on college campuses" while only 12 percent of the teenagers felt this way. On the second question, we find 22 percent of the over-60s saying that coverage of "riots and protest in the streets" is a change for the better, compared with 58 percent of the under-20s. Even when controlled by the usually dominant variable of education, these sharp differences held up.

In 1980, there were no mass movements like civil rights or war protest to so clearly engage the attention and participation of young people and nothing to place in our questionnaire that would so sharply split the age groups. The closest we come to it is with a few questions that might evoke responses along a liberal-conservative dimension. The results of three of these, all having to do with approval or disapproval of ways in which television has changed, are shown in table 3.4. There is a small but uniform relationship with age on these three items. Young people, especially those in their teens or twenties, are more apt to give the liberal

Table 3.4 Reactions to Changes in Television During Last 10 Years by Age

	Percent Saying "Change for the Better"			
AGE	More Open Treatment of Sex	More Open Treatment of Drugs & Race Relations	More Programs with Blacks in Important Roles	(N)
18–19	29	71	70	(94)
20–29	32	73	65	(397)
30–39	24	72	64	(342)
40–49	23	72	65	(280)
50–59	14	70	60	(258)
60+	13	66	59	(382)

response of a "change for the better." Those over 50 take a more conservative position.

These age differences are certainly not dramatic, nor were any very pronounced differences among age groups found elsewhere in the 1980 questionnaires. Slightly more of the young thought that television should provide more information about national campaigns and political candidates and slightly more of them approved television coverage of the Iranian crisis, but the large generational gap seen in 1970 did not reappear.

The Public Television Audience

Public television (PTV), previously called "educational television" has grown far more rapidly than television broadcasting as a whole over the past thirty years. In 1960, when Gary Steiner conducted his study, there were 44 educational TV stations in operation, with an audience so small that it did not merit comment in the Steiner report. At that time, a third of the stations broadcast on ultrahigh frequences (UHF) (above channel 13), which many of the sets were not equipped to receive. Following the 1964 ruling that manufacturers must equip new sets with UHF receivers, our 1970 study found about half the population able to receive some public station.

The number of stations had grown to 184 (106 UHF and 78 VHF) and the audience had reached an estimated 24 million viewers per week. Lyle's (1975) estimate in *The People Look at Public Television* (written for the Corporation for Public Broadcasting) was that up to 80 percent of the households were able to reach one of the 245 public stations then broadcasting. In our 1980 study, 87 percent of the respondents said they could receive one of the public stations. In that year there were 272 such stations, 38 percent of which broadcast on VHF. As for the rest of the stations virtually, all sets in use were equipped to receive UHF signals.

In total size, the actual audience for PTV has kept pace with its availability, but the composition of this audience remains very unevenly spread among various segments of the population. It is, in fact, a consistent finding of studies that have been conducted on the subject that the audience of public television is disproportionately well-educated. (Schramm, Lyle, Pool 1963; Lyle 1975; Comstock et al. 1978.) Our 1970 investigation found that there were two reasons for the greater viewing among the better educated. They were more apt to live in areas that were served by PTV stations and to have sets that could receive their signals; in addition, they were more inclined to tune in. The 1970 findings are shown in table 3.5 along with the comparable 1980 figures.

Table 3.5 Viewing of Public Television, by Education

	Can Receive a PTV (ETV) Station		Watch "Ever"		Watch Once-a-Week or More		Number of Cases	
Education	1970	1980	1970	1980	1970	1980	1970	1980
Grade school	27	73	16	46	6	27	(345)	(230)
High school	51	82	32	58	18	42	(1011)	(1087)
College	63	91	48	77	33	64	(480)	(679)
Total	50	87	33	63	20	48	(1836)	(1996)

The table shows a 1980 audience of adult once-a-week viewers that is both larger (48 percent versus the 20 percent in 1970) and more evenly spread among education groups than was found ten years before. The college-educated contingent now out-views those with only grade school education by about 2-to-1, compared to the 5.5-to-1 of 1970. But the two sources of the discrepancy remain. The less educated are still less able to receive a PTV station and when they can view it are less apt to do so. The latter point is demonstrated in figure 3.8, where the characteristics of the PTV audience are shown in relation to several variables, based on the 87 percent of the population that can receive PTV. As can be seen, there are considerably more viewers among the college-educated, even when we eliminate those who cannot receive PTV from the calculations.

The other characteristic that would appear to influence viewing is parenthood. Those parents with children living at home

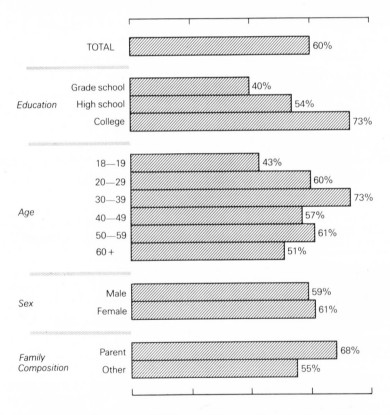

FIGURE 3.8. Viewing of PTV Once a Week or More by Those Who Can Receive It.

view considerably more than others, and the high proportion of viewers in their thirties is largely a reflection of the fact that people of that age in our sample are more likely to have children living at home.

Pursuing the idea that children's viewing of public television might influence their elders, we asked parents about the viewing of other members of the household, with resulting findings that reflect the increased audiences of PTV in general. Only 10 percent of the parents in 1980 said that no one else in the household watched, down from 35 percent in 1970, and 72 percent said that one or more of their children watched at least once a week, up from 58 percent ten years earlier. Aside from this general trend toward increased viewing among children, the only thing that seemed to change a bit was the amount of viewing by parents related to the age of children. In 1970, the heavy parent audience was among those with children under five; in 1980, those with children over five were making a better showing, as can be seen in figure 3.9. Our number of cases is too few and the mixture of children's ages among the

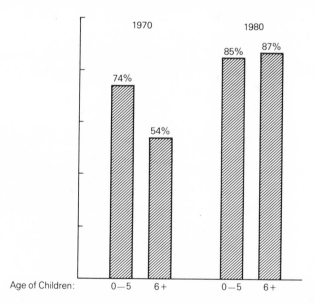

FIGURE 3.9. Parents' Viewing (One a Week or More) by Ages of Children

families in the sample is too diverse to permit any very definite conclusions, but tentatively these findings suggest a shift away from the *Sesame Street* contingent as the influentials in household viewing patterns and toward the older siblings. And, perhaps, the audience is generally growing older as the content of PTV alters. The 1970's, for example, brought more PTV programming for the older siblings, such as *Electric Company* and *3-2-1 Contact.*

The greater attention of the better-educated to PTV is consistent with the attitudes expressed by various education groups toward that sector of television broadcasting. Whereas enthusiam for commercial television in general decreases with education, with respect to PTV the more favorable attitudes are found among the better-educated (Lyle 1975; Hart 1979; Roper 1981). Peter Hart, in a study among likely voters in several states, found that college graduates were far more likely than those without high school degrees to rate PTV "excellent" or "good" (73 percent to 46 percent), and to agree with the statement: "The people who run public television have my best interests at heart" (71 percent to 41 percent). The better educated were also more likely to feel that it would make "a great deal of difference" if there were no public television (39 percent to 16 percent). Roper, in a more recent survey, finds 45 percent of the college-educated rating public television as "generally good," compared with 34 percent of the high-school graduates and 26 percent of those with a grade-school education.

Though we avoided direct comparisons between commercial and public television in our own 1970 and 1980 studies, so as to maintain compatibility with Gary Steiner's original approach, we do find in both studies a general attitude expressed by the better-educated about what is desirable in television programming that fits the public model better than it does the commercial. When asked what sorts of programs they would like to see more of, or less of, 77 percent of the college-educated said there are not enough educational programs for adults, compared with 60 percent of those with high-school education and 47 percent of the grade-school contingent. Table 3.6 shows the result of another question which asks the respondents to choose between two broad types of pro-

Table 3.6
"Generally speaking, would you say that television should do more in the way of providing information material, or should it concentrate on providing the best entertainment possible?"

Education	By Education			
	Information	Entertainment	Both, Can't Choose	(N)
Grade school	21	45	34	(230)
High school	28	40	32	(1087)
College	39	21	40	(679)

Table 3.7 Choice of Television Among the Four Mass Media, by Education

Education	"Presents Things the Most Intelligently"	"Is the Most Educational"	"Gives the Clearest Under-standing of Elections"	(N)
Grade school	71	70	81	(230)
High school	53	58	69	(1087)
College	31	41	46	(679)

Table 3.8 Percent Agreeing with Two Statements, by Education

Education	"I Watch to Learn Something"	"Commercials Help Keep Me Informed"	(N)
Grade school	39	59	(230)
High school	28	53	(1087)
College	21	37	(679)

gramming. Predictably, it is the college group that said it wants information more than entertainment.

As might be surmised from such findings, and from data presented previously, a major criticism of the better-educated viewers is that television is not sufficiently informational or educational or generally cerebral—a point on which they disagree with their less educated fellow viewers to a large extent. The least educated of our subgroups, those with a grade-school education, tend to find much in the normal fare of television that informs and educates. Tables 3.7 and 3.8 present some pertinent findings. When asked to compare the mass media on various counts, 71 percent of the grade-school-educated choose television as the medium that "presents things most intelligently," compared with 31 percent of the college educated (table 3.7). Seventy percent of the gradeschoolers think television "is the most educational," as do 21 percent of the college crowd; and for 81 percent of the grade-school-educated television gives the "clearest understanding of the candidates and issues in national elections." Television is chosen by 46 percent of the college-educated on that item. In table 3.8, we see that the less educated are also far more likely to say they watch television "to learn something" and to express the view that even commercials help to keep them informed. The population divides along educational lines in regard to entertainment versus the educational functions of television more than on practically anything else. The educated viewer tells us he feels that television in general provides too little of information and should have more, and he has a high regard for PTV, which he watches increasingly, but still not very much. His less educated counterpart feels the opposite to a considerable degree and hardly watches public television at all.

It is particularly the less educated viewer, who demonstrates in our surveys how much people think they may learn from television. But even before television became the dominant medium there was evidence of educational effects garnered over 40 years of research on the electronic media. Early work of the sort that was later called "uses and gratifications research" showed that female listeners to radio soap operas in the early 1940s were receiving what they believed to be useful information on how to deal with the day-to-day problems of life at home (Herzog 1944). Since then, a host of other studies have shown the ways in which television may educate. There have been studies comparing the effectiveness of television versus personal presentation in the classroom (Chu and Schramm 1975), further work in the needs and gratification tradition pointing to information derived as a gratified need (Katz et al. 1973), studies suggesting the efficacy of television in presenting the case for political candidates (Blumler and McQuail 1969), and studies showing a variety of educational effects (Himmelweit, 1958; Schramm, et al. 1961), including the improvement in ability to get along with the oppositie sex among teenagers (Gerson, 1966; Greenberg & Dervin, 1971). Recently, we find a suggestion of learning in studies stemming from some newer conceptions of television's influence in the modern world—that it "sets the agenda" for social and political thought, establishing what's important (Weaver et al. 1981) or that it "cultivates" by providing its viewers with an image of the world, real or created (Gerbner et al. 1977). It is not within the scope of this inquiry to judge the quality or the effectiveness of the education derived from either commerical or public television. It is appropriate to point out, however, that a considerable amount of the education is *thought* to be derived from both—for the less educated, particularly from commercial television and for the better educated, particularly from PTV.

The amount of time spent watching public television is still very small (a very rough estimate from our own data would put it at about 3 percent of total adult viewing time) but there seems no doubt that it is increasing apace, especially among the less educated. The main cause for the increase is the spread of its availability around the country, but at the same time the content of both commercial television and public television have been undergoing gradual changes. This could be a cause of the larger PTV audience, or a result, or a combination of both. As noted in chapter 2, the commercial TV programs that could be placed in the category of 'news, information, and public affairs' have more than doubled since 1960, and some feel that the quality of the entertainment programming has here and there taken on a more intellectual tone (for example in programs like *Roots*) and has displayed more sensitivity to human values (*Mash, Hill Street Blues*). At the same time—or at least since 1970, when it started to have a perceptible audience—the instructional content of public television programming has declined as a proportion of the total. (By "instructional" content is meant *Sesame Street* and *The Electric Company* as well as programs designed for classroom use.) The category that the Corporation for Public Broadcasting calls "general" has increased proportionally. "General" includes "news and public affairs," "information skills," of which *Nova* and *The Adams Chronicles* are examples, as well as some other program types. General programming increased from 61 percent to 72 percent of the total (table

Table 3.9 Public Television Program Content

| | Percent of Total Hours | |
	1974	1980
Instructional	(17)	(13)
Sesame Street & Electric Company	(21)	(16)
General		
News & Public Affairs	13	12
Information Skills	16	23
Cultural	18	22
General Children's	11	9
Other	4	6
Total General	(62)	(72)

SOURCE: Katzman 1975, Katzman & Katzman 1982.

3.9). In relative terms, commercial television is moving a bit toward the interests of a better-educated population and public television is moving a bit toward the habitual viewing of a broader audience. In the process, the distinction between the two, which is still considerable, is becoming just a bit blurred along the edges.

The Black Audience

We noted above that race accounts for the largest proportion of the variance in attitudes toward television when 13 variables are subjected to multivariate analysis. This attitudinal difference is shown rather more dramatically by a look at the proportions among the two races who choose the most favorable positions on the items that make up the attitude scale—the superfans. Table 3.10 gives these proportions for the three surveys. The overall decline in the proportions of superfans from 1960 to 1980 is noticeable for both blacks and whites, but the difference between the races persists over the two decades, with the black proportion of enthusiasts exceeding the white by a good 2-to-1. The greater regard for television of the black audience is also seen when we tabulate the attitude scores by education levels as in table 3.11. In each of the surveys and at each educational level, the blacks score higher (more

Table 3.10 Percent Taking the Most Favorable Position on Six-Point Scale, by Race

	1960		1970		1980	
	White	Black	White	Black	White	Black
Television is:						
Exciting	26	63	15	58	13	39
In good taste	21	49	14	56	10	36
Important	36	63	26	65	20	52
Excellent	19	44	12	43	9	22
Relaxing	41	56	29	62	20	41
Interesting	39	64	28	61	21	47
Wonderful	23	60	14	58	10	26
For me	37	65	24	58	19	47
Getting better	23	45	12	46	8	34
Informative	37	57	32	61	24	53
Base: 100% =	(1949)	(247)	(1710)	(190)	(1677)	(248)

Table 3.11 Attitude Scores, by Race and Education

	Grade School		High School		College	
	Score	(N)	Score	(N)	Score	(N)
1960						
White	24	(465)	23	(1031)	19	(453)
Black	27	(102)	26	(113)	23	(32)
1970						
White	24	(287)	22	(912)	19	(459)
Black	28	(66)	28	(99)	27	(24)
1980						
White	22	(147)	20	(914)	17	(616)
Black	28	(64)	26	(146)	22	(38)

favorable) on the scale running from 0 to 35, than do their white counterparts. The evidence of favorable predispositions among the black audience thus persists both over time and when the effects of other important variables, such as education level, are controlled. Blacks like TV more than white people do.

Another characteristic of the black audience is its defiance of some of the regularities of TV audience behavior to which most communication researchers have become accustomed. Traditionally, the uses of communications are found to be closely related to the socioeconomic status of the user; those on the higher levels use print and the lower level use radio, television, or word-of-mouth. Of the measurable elements that compose socioeconomic status (income, education, style of housing, social class affiliation, etc.), Steiner, and many before and after him, found educational level to be the best single predictor of how the population uses and reacts to television. But blacks don't always follow the general rules. In our 1970 study we observed, and reported somewhat hesitantly, that the better educated black members of the sample seemed to hold a relatively high regard for the medium and to view it even more frequently than the less educated blacks.

One of the 1970 findings is reproduced in table 3.12, with the 1980 figures added. It shows the proportion of whites and blacks at each educational level who report that they are likely to watch evening and weekend television 35 or more hours a week—the heavy viewers. In both 1970 and 1980, the highest proportion of black heavy viewers is found among the better educated. In the second survey, the high-school graduates have twice the proportion of heavy viewers of the gradeschoolers, and the college-educated a quarter more than the highschoolers.

Another question used in all three surveys asked whether the respondent thought he was spending too much time watching TV or didn't see "as much as you would like to see" (table 3.13). As viewing has been increasing, the overall proportions of the samples choosing the second of these alternatives ("would like to see more") has been going down, in reasonably accommodation to satisfied aspirations. But note that in all cases a higher proportion of blacks feel that they want to see more and that the black college group expresses that wish in 1980 even more than they had in 1960 (39 percent to 32 percent), during a period when viewing was going

Table 3.12 Amount of Viewing (Proportion of "Heavy" Viewers) (In Percent)

	1970				1980			
	White		Black		White		Black	
Education	%	(N)	%	(N)	%	(N)	%	(N)
Grade school	40	(287)	29	(66)	24	(163)	19	(68)
High school	33	(912)	37	(99)	32	(936)	37	(157)
College	29	(459)	48	(24)	24	(654)	46	(39)
Total %	33	(1658)	37	(189)	28	(1753)	34	(264)

Table 3.13 Percent That Would Like to See More TV, by Race and Education

Education	1960 White	1960 Black	1970 White	1970 Black	1980 White	1980 Black
Grade school	31	49	16	27	10	20
High school	24	30	21	41	15	27
College	15	32	14	41	9	39
Total%	25	38	18	38	12	27
Base 100% =	(1951)	(287)	(1662)	(191)	(1679)	(249)

up and enthusiasm for the medium was going down. Insofar as answers to this question are in any way predictive of viewing in the future, television seems more likely to maintain its educated black audience than most any other group.

The 1980 national study also reveals that blacks (more than whites) watch television for what they can learn from it and use it for communication with family and friends. The sample members were presented with a long list of "reasons" for watching and asked to say how often each applied to their viewing (usually, occasionally, rarely, or never). The two items on which there was the greatest difference between the races were: "I watch because I think I can learn something" ("usually" for whites 25 percent and for blacks 45 percent), and "I watch because everyone I know is watching and I want to be able to talk about it afterwards" ("usually" for whites 5 percent and for blacks 25 percent). Other studies have shown that practical education ranks high with blacks among reasons for viewing. Dervin and Greenberg (1972), for instance, find that a high proportion of a low-income urban black sample agree that people watch TV for such reasons as "they can learn a lot" (73 percent) and, "they can learn from the mistakes of others" (69 percent). From such answers it is hard to tell whether the learning is thought to come from the entertainment features which blacks, like whites, watch more than anything else, or from the news and documentary programs. We do know that blacks, more than whites at the same educational level, tend to rely on the appreciate TV as a news medium, when compared to other media. Sixty-seven percent of our 1980 black sample choose television over radio, magazines, and newspapers and the medium that "gives the most complete news coverage" (50 percent for whites) and 69 percent chose it over the other media as the "most educational" (49 percent for whites). Other researchers have noted this reliance of blacks on televsion for news and information. Comstock et al. (1978) consider that "the shift of blacks toward television as a news source is a major phenomenon of audience behavior of the past decade." As we have noted above, the shift toward television for news and information takes place among all elements of the population, but it has indeed been most pronounced among the blacks.

It would propably be a mistake, however, to assume that all the information which blacks find so useful comes from the news and documentary programs (which blacks list among their favorite programs slightly less than whites). The 25 percent of the blacks may not have the news in mind when saying, as noted above, they watch because "they want to talk about it afterwards." It could just as well have been a basketball game or an episode in a comedy series. Similarly, when Walter Gerson (1966) found that black teenagers were more apt than their white counterparts to use the mass media for "ideas and advice" about dating, it is unlikely that the referent was national or international news for either race. The Gerson study suggests that blacks in particular find hints for daily life in the less pedagogical fare on TV, but perhaps not just in the entertainment programs. When we asked as series of agree-disagree questions about TV advertising, far more of the black sample than of the white agreed with the statement "I find some commercials very helpful in keeping me informed" by a margin of 79 percent to 44 percent.

As noted before, blacks as a group are often seen as conforming, in patterns of behavior and attitude, to the norms of the white population of lower socioeconomic status. To some small extent, the model seems to fit—blacks as a group do share with less-educated whites a great admiration for commercial television and both groups see it as a primary source of information. But still, it is hard to embrace the model warmly when we see a variable like amount of education acting in a reverse fashion for blacks and whites. We suspect that the nonconforming nature of the blacks may be a consequence of the discrimination that they have experienced in American society. Interracial attitudes, and not too long ago state and local governmental policies, have restricted participation of our black viewers in many facets of society, but television permits a vicarious participation which they cannot be denied. The fact that most of the content of commercial television is of middle class orientation, often representing in the entertainment programs situations in which blacks may feel most deprived, would make it seem somewhat reasonable that blacks of upper socioeconomic status would watch, and express the desire to watch even more, to a greater extent than others, including the less-educated blacks.

The Cable Audience

One of the more dramatic developments in the television industry during the course of our studies has been the spread of cable TV, available to practically none of the U.S. households in 1960, to about 5 percent in 1970, and to 23 percent in 1980. The expansion continues. Has cable, with extra channels and pay TV options, created a different sort of audience? In this section, we examine findings from the most recent study on the reasons for acquiring cable, the sorts of people who have acquired it, and some of the differences and similarities between the cable users and the rest of the television audience.

About half (51 percent) of the cable users in our 1980 sample had been subscribers for three years or less, 25 percent of them for less than a year—in accord with the recent rapid expansion of the facilities. When asked "what was your main reason for getting cable?" many of the respondents gave more than one answer and at least half expressed the desire for more variety, either through the addition of channels that they could not receive without cable or through better reception of channels that could otherwise be seen only dimly. A number of respondents mentioned some aspect of programming that they thought might be augmented by cable— more sports (8 percent), more movies (5 percent), programs without commercials (7 percent), and Home Box Office (3 percent). Practically no one said they need cable in order to watch television at all, which suggests that cable has generally augmented the viewing opportunities for those who were already members of the audience rather than recruiting new members.

It is in line with such motivations as "better reception," "more channels," and "more variety" that the main factors distinguishing cable users from others would be geographic. They live in places where reception is limited. It is also reasonable to assume that cable TV companies would seek to establish their local facilities where the need was felt and also where there was enough concentration of demand to make the effort of wiring individual households and building local relay stations economically feasible. In a multivariate analysis using the previously identified 13 variables (see chapter 2) as predictors of cable subscription, size of place and region of the country, in that order, showed up as the factors that explained much better than others who is apt to have cable. In respect to population concentration, only 3 percent of the people in the cities of over 1 million and 17 percent of those in cities between 100,000 and 1 million had cable. However, 37 percent of the sample members living in the urban fringes around the metropolitan centers, and 63 percent of those living in open country, had cable. The "urban fringes" and "open country," however, tend to be those in regions of the country that are quite well populated and where the distance between households is relatively small. Among the regional divisions defined by the U.S. census, the highest concentration of cable households is in the Mid-Atlantic states (New York, New Jersey, and Pennsylvania); 44 percent of our sample living in the region subscribe to cable. That contrasts with 9 percent of those living in the South East Central states (Kentucky, Tennessee, Alabama, and Mississippi) and 7 percent of those living in the eight Rocky Mountain states, from Montana in the north to New Mexico in the south. Cable is thus concentrated in the *least* populous parts of the *most* populous areas.

Some of the other factors that appear to distinguish the cable users may also, in part, be a consequence of location. The one personal characteristic that markedly separates the two groups is race. Twenty-six percent of the whites in the sample have cable but only 8 percent of the blacks (see table 3.14). Very likely this is mainly a result of the concentration of blacks in large cities which have a low penetration of cable and in some rural areas where the wiring for cable is not economically viable. The fact that race turns up in the multivariate analysis as a factor explaining a significant amount of the variance, however, suggests that there may be other unknown reasons for blacks' less enthusiastic response to the opportunity to subscribe—perhaps greater satisfaction with what is already available. Even with allowance made for location, income, occupation, and several other variables, fewer blacks have cable. Overall, the multivariate analysis shows that size of place, region, race, age, and income, in combination, account for 21.4 percent of the total variance.

Among the white, education makes some difference, with the very poorly educated, who are apt also to be older and perhaps more old-fashioned, showing significantly less adoption of cable. Income and occupation make relatively little difference, but whether or not there are children in the household does have some effect. The households with children are more apt to have cable

Table 3.14 Proportion of Cable Households, Among Selected Population Groups

	Percent	No. of Cases
RACE		
White	26	1769
Black	8	265
EDUCATION (White Only)		
Grade school	19	159
High school	28	926
College	26	633
FAMILY INCOME (White Only)		
Under $7,000	22	124
7,000–14,999	26	305
15,000–24,999	29	462
25,000 and over	30	390
HOUSEHOLD COMPOSITION (White Only)		
With children	31	609
Without	25	907
OCCUPATION, IF EMPLOYED (White Only)		
White collar	25	413
Blue collar	27	791

than those without, by 31 percent to 25 percent—perhaps because there are more appetites to satisfy.

An examination of data on attitudes toward television suggests that cable users have not acquired the new facility because of an unusually high regard for the medium in general, nor have they developed a greater fondness as a result of their experience with cable. The attitude scores for cable and noncable TV viewers, as measured by the scale shown in chapter 2, are almost precisely the same. The average attitude score is 20.5 for the cable users and 20.8 for the others. On another question, also shown in chapter 2, when the respondents were asked which they would keep of items available in most households if they could have only one, 40 percent of the cable users chose TV as a first, second, or third choice compared with 44 percent of those without cable. On the other hand, cable use appears to have some relationship to the way people go about selecting the programs they watch—if only a modest one. From answers to a question on the selection methods used, to be shown in the next chapter, it appears that the cable users are somewhat more apt to read such publications as *TV Guide* then the non-users (59 percent for those with cable, 51 percent for those without) and more likely to read the listings in the daily newspaper (25 percent to 20 percent).

In another respect, too, they differ somewhat from those without cable—they have more heavy viewers in their camp. Thirty-two percent of the cable subscribers in our sample report watching more than 35 hours a week. The proportion of heavy viewers among those without cable is 28 percent. As with heavy viewers generally, the selection of programs to watch goes a bit more to "light entertainment" fare (table 3.15). In response to the question "what are some of your favorite programs—those you watch regularly or whenever you get a chance?"—75 percent of the programs mentioned by the cable users were in the light entertainment area, compared with 69 percent for those without cable. The latter were more apt to mention news and information programs (27 percent to 20 percent).

Similarly, when asked whether television should provide more "information material" or should concentrate on "the best

Table 3.15
"What are some of your favorite programs—those you watch regularly or whenever you get a chance?"

	With Cable (%)	Without Cable (%)
Light Entertainment	(75)	(69)
Comedy/Variety	23	26
Movies	5	3
Action	6	8
Sports	10	7
Light Music	2	1
Light Drama	29	24
News and Information	(20)	(27)
Regular News	5	9
Information and Public Affairs	15	18
Heavy Drama	(—)	(1)
Religion	(2)	(1)
Classical Music	(—)	(—)
Other	(3)	(2)
N =	(466)	(1515)

entertainment," the cable users were 30 percent for information, 33 percent for entertainment, and 38 percent for "both." Those without cable voted 32 percent for information, 33 percent for entertainment, and 36 percent for both. On one other question 77 percent of the cable users report watching public television at least once a week, 78 percent of those without. Overall, the differences in program selection appear quite small.

The answer to the question posed at the beginning of this section—has cable produced a different sort of television audience—is more *no* than *yes*. There are some differences in the sorts of people who subscribe to cable and those who don't, but those differences are largely geographic, resulting from the accident of living in areas where cable systems are available. The cable users feel the same way about television in general as do the others. They watch a bit more, but the types of programs they like to watch are very similar.

CHAPTER FOUR

What the Audience Wants and Doesn't Want

T his chapter deals with some of the more speculative features of the three studies–questions about what people seem to like and dislike about the content of television; about how they evaluate the changes that have taken place in the medium over the past twenty years; about why they watch as much as they do; and about how their attitudes correspond, or don't correspond, with their actual viewing. We start with some questions used in the 1970 and 1980 surveys to tap the public's reactions to the changes that had taken place in broadcasting during the prior decade.

Perception of Changes

When the 1970 sample was asked to say what they saw as important changes that had taken place in television during the 1960s, the increase in news and information was noted by more respondents (33 percent of the sample) than any other aspect. Next in order, mentioned by 23 percent of the sample, were various technological changes of the 1960s, such as the spread of color TV, satellite broadcasting, and the greater number of receivable educational channels. A smaller number (10 percent) mentioned morality themes—more sex, nudity, vulgarity—and a still smaller number (4 percent) an increase in violence. Two types of entertainment programs that people saw to be on the increase were singled out for attention—sports programs by 5 percent and movies by 7 percent. All-in-all, the changes that most people said they noticed corresponded quite well with the changes that had actually occurred in television broadcasting during the decade.

In 1980, when the question was asked again, the answers were distributed as shown in table 4.1. Comments about news and

Table 4.1
"Now, how about changes that have taken place in TV over the past ten
years? What do you see as some of the important changes that have taken
place?"

| | | Direction of Mentions | | |
Mentions	Total Percent Mentioning	Favorable	Unfavorable	Neither, Neutral, Unspecified
More news and information	23	59%	2%	39%
More sex	17	1	56	43
Violence (mostly more)	13	2	50	48
Technical changes	11	62	1	37
More sports	9	36	5	59
"Moral standards"	8	—	62	38
Movies (mostly more)	6	46	9	45
Explicit treatment of various subjects	3	21	18	62
Children's shows (more)	2	37	7	57
Base: 100% =	(2031)			
Base for evaluation varies from 41 to 465.				

public affairs programming—more coverage, better coverage, more
local news programs—again led the list of observed changes, but
this time were noticed by 23 percent rather than 33 percent of the
sample. News was followed by two features of TV programming that
received considerably more attention than in 1970. Seventeen percent of the sample felt that sex was being more openly portrayed
on the screen than it had been before; for example:

> There's nothing left unsaid or undone anymore on TV. They were
> told to take sex out of the bedroom and they just put it in the
> livingroom.

> Sex and more sex. There is more sex in advertising, things like
> women's bra ads. I think they are unnecessary. The daytime
> series are sex-oriented.

> Ten years ago they didn't use any bad language. Now they use
> it all day long and don't think nothing about it. They dress inde-
> cently and everybody jumps in bed with everybody else. I think
> it's just awful.

The second feature noticed was violence, which the public felt to be on the increase since 1970. The proportion of these noticing a higher level of violence increased from 4 to 13 percent, with comments such as:

> There's a lot more violence and murders. It's all around. The violence and sex attitudes, and the deterioration of morals. [Television] has gone to the bottom.

Changes in the technology of television broadcasting were mentioned by 11 percent, less than half the proportion that had noted them previously. The 1980 sample noticed especially the spread of cable, which was indeed one of the more pronounced industry advances during the decade.

In general, the 1980 population liked far less the changes they noticed of the seventies than had the 1970 population the changes of the sixties. Table 4.2 is a summary of the results for both years by coding the overall direction of the replies—approving of the changes that had been noticed, disapproving of them or neutral. The 1970 sample members were predominantly in favor of the changes they had noticed, reflecting the high regard people felt for the emergence of television journalism and for the technical advances of the decade. In 1980, the emphases on morality themes resulted in a split decision—23 percent approving and 21 percent disapproving.

The separate views that many of the public hold about television entertainment and television news may also explain the differences found in the answers to two other questions asked in 1970 and 1980, shown in table 4.3. The 1980 survey found twice as

Table 4.2

"Now, how about changes that have taken place in TV over the past ten years? What do you see as some of the important changes that have taken place?"

Overall Direction of Reply	1970	1980
Favorable	55	23
Unfavorable	16	21
Balanced, neutral	14	37
Don't know/NA	15	19
Base: 100% =	(2000)	(2078)

Table 4.3

"How about the entertainment programs during the evening after 7:30 as compared to ten years ago. Do you think they have got better, worse, or stayed about the same?"

	Percent Who Say:	
	1970	1980
Better	48	40
Worse	12	25
Stayed the same	32	28
Don't know	8	7
Base: 100% =	(1849)	(2030)

"Compared to ten years ago, do you think that the way the news is presented on TV is generally better or generally worse, or has it stayed about the same?"

Better	69	66
Worse	7	7
Stayed the same	19	22
Don't know	5	6
Base: 100% =	(1855)	(2039)

many respondents thinking that entertainment programs were getting worse than had been found in 1970 (25 percent to 12 percent). No such change took place in the answers to a comparable question on news programs. Almost as many respondents in 1980 thought that they were getting better as had thought so ten years earlier (66 percent to 69 percent).

In addition to these questions, the 1980 respondents were presented with a list of fourteen changes in commercial broadcasting during the seventies that had been noted by a panel of network researchers. In table 4.4 are the answers to two questions that were asked about each item. Had the respondent noticed it, and if so did he think that it was a change for the better or a change for the worse? Only one item was thought to be a "change for the worse." In line with the morality theme that appeared in response to the open-ended question discussed above, 66 percent thought that "more open treatment of sex" was a change for the worse, compared with 21 percent who considered it a change for the better. That change was also one of the more widely noticed—by 88 percent of the sample. All the other changes listed in table 4.4 received the approval of a wide margin of those who noticed them, from 89-to-

Table 4.4

"Here are some ways people have noticed that TV has changed over the past ten years. Would you read down the list and tell me whether it is a change you have noticed or not?"

As far as your own viewing is concerned, has this been a change for the better, a change for the worse, or hasn't it made any difference to you?

	Percent Noticed Change	Of Those Who Noticed			
		Change for Better	Change for Worse	No Differ- ence	Don't Know
More women presenting the news	91	65	6	27	2
More open treatment of sex on TV	88	21	66	9	4
More programs with blacks in important roles	87	61	10	26	3
More open treatment of problems like drugs and race relations	85	67	22	6	4
The "advisories" or "warnings" that are sometimes given at the start of programs	79	89	3	8	1
Movies made especially for TV	78	71	9	17	2
Women taking more important roles in entertainment programs	76	72	4	23	1
More live sports programs especially in the evening	73	62	17	19	2
More light conversation among members of local news teams	69	57	19	22	2
Reruns of old series from previous years	64	49	23	27	1
More time devoted to local news programs	64	82	7	11	0
Mini series programs in prime time	63	71	10	17	2
More substitution of specials for the regular programs	60	62	14	22	2
Greater variety of programs in late evening	28	71	8	19	2
Base 100% =	(2045)				
Base for evaluations varies from 590–1885.					

3 for "program advisories" to 49-to-23 for "returns of old programs." It is noteworthy that the other changes relating to national social issues—"women presenting the news," "blacks in more important roles," "programs on drugs and race relations," and "women taking more important roles" all received the pronounced endorsement of the public.

In 1970 we used a similar question to obtain reactions

Table 4.5 Percent with High Approval of Changes by Education

	1970		1980	
	%	(N)	%	(N)
Grade school	18	(368)	24	(215)
High school	31	(1030)	25	(1103)
College	40	(490)	22	(670)

to changes in television that had occurred during the sixties—more educational channels, satellite broadcasts, on-the-spot coverage of Vietnam, color TV, and so forth. Of course the questions are not directly comparable for the two surveys, but one analytic comparison may still be made. It appeared in 1970 that the observed changes were of the sort to receive the resounding endorsement of the better-educated members of the sample; the less-educated were considerably less enthusiastic. In table 4.5 are shown the proportions for each educational group of high-approvers—those who scored highest on a scale developed from "change for better," "change for worse," or "no difference" answers to the observed changes. As can be seen, the 1970 college-educated contingent had a considerably higher proportion of high scorers than the gradeschoolers (40 percent to 18 percent). The better-educated, who found more to dislike about television than others, nontheless thought that it was changing in the right direction during the sixties. They particularly approved the more extensive news coverage that the medium was providing. Deliberately or not, television appears to have been catering to the interests of the better-educated citizens. But not so, we find, during the seventies. Table 4.5 also shows the 1980 proportion of high approval of changes. The high-approvers are distributed rather evenly among the three educational groups. Undoubtedly the slowdown in the seventies of the previous decade's remarkable expansion of TV journalism (see chapter 5) is at least part of the answer.

The Biggest Moment

Among the various means Steiner used in 1960 to discover what it was in television that so appealed to the public was a question he posed about people's most memorable moment before the set:

Considering everything you've seen on television is there some
highlight or special moment that stands out in your mind? It can
be either a whole program or event or something that happened
during a program—just anything that impressed you. What was
it?

As noted in our previous report, most of the 1960 respondents who
had any answers to the question mentioned entertainment programs or episodes in entertainment programs (24 percent). A
smaller number, some 15 percent, mentioned events covered by
news cameras (table 4.6). By 1970 "big moments" of entertainment
were down to 5 percent and news coverage accounted for almost all
the remaining mentions (52 percent). It is possible that the new
question wording used in 1970 and 1980 (see table 4.6) was responsible for some of the shift away from entertainment, but it is more
likely that the increased attention given to the news features of
television, to be discussed in the next chapter, is the major factor,
along with the dramatic events that the cameras were able to cover,
such as President Kennedy's assassination and the explorations in
space. News continued to dominate the "big moments" into 1980,

Table 4.6
1960: "Considering everything you've ever seen on television, is there some
highlight or special moment that stands out in your mind? It can be either a
whole program or event or something that happened during a program—
just anything that impressed you. What was it?"
1970, 1980: "Can you think of the one biggest moment on television for
you—one time you would have missed TV the most if you could not have
watched what was on? What was it?"

	Percent		
Answers	1960	1970	1980
No, can't think of any	48	42	53
Episodes in entertainment series	24	5	5
News coverage of special events	15	52	24
JFK assassination	—	(12)	(7)
Space shots	—	(35)	(9)
Pope's visit	—	(—)	(2)
Other	—	(5)	(6)
Specials and Documentaries	13	1	7
Olympics	—	—	2
Other Sports Events	—	—	8
Base: 100% =	(2427)	(1900)	(2078)

but with more of the memories going to sports events like Olympics and Super Bowls. If the medium was somewhat less memorable for its news coverage, it could be that events seemed less dramatic to the viewing public during the seventies.

Viewer Preferences

An account of what sorts of programs the public thought television should provide was central to Steiner's inquiry in 1960. He asked "what do you want" in a variety of ways, including a series of questions on the sorts of programs that presumably fill various audience needs—to laugh, to be informed, to escape. Were there enough, not enough, or too many of each sort of program? Most of these questions were also used in the 1970 and 1980 replications, with additions here and there for new program types that appeared. The three survey results are shown in table 4.7.

Here Steiner discovered one of those interesting anomalies that stud his work. Those relaxed viewers of 1960 who had depicted television as a hedonistic refuge by and large now said that it should provide more educational programs. As we can see from the various items in the table, the 1960 audience appears satisfied with the supply of programs for escape and laughs—the majority said there were enough of these—but nearly two-thirds thought that educational programs were in short supply. Expressions of this point of view persisted in the two subsequent surveys.

To allay the suspicion that those who advised on the need for more educational programs were really thinking of *Sesame Street* and other fare designed for children, we asked two additional questions in 1980 separating educational programs for children from those for adults. The results are shown in table 4.7. The conclusion is that our 1980 respondents meant both; there were not enough educational programs either for children or for adults. For children, the types of programs most frequently thought to be in short supply were the well-known products of public television. A few respondents mention fare more often found on commercial

Table 4.7

"Television programs can be designed to provide different things. From your point of view, does television have enough, not enough, or too many of each of these kinds of programs?"

Kind of Program	1960	1970	1980
EDUCATION			
Enough	34	24	31
Not enough	65	75	68
Too many	1	1	1
	(1517)	(1517)	(1786)
ESCAPE FROM EVERYDAY LIFE			
Enough	74	56	61
Not enough	11	17	14
Too many	15	27	25
	(1143)	(1343)	(1749)
ADVICE ON PROBLEM SOLVING			
Enough	61	35	36
Not enough	32	58	58
Too many	6	7	6
	(1096)	(1008)	(1419)
JUST LAUGHS			
Enough	63	61	62
Not enough	31	32	28
Too many	5	8	9
	(1161)	(1710)	(1924)
INFORMATION ABOUT POLITICS AND POLITICAL CANDIDATES			
Enough	—	57	59
Not enough	—	26	26
Too many	—	18	16
		(1474)	(1898)
EDUCATIONAL PROGRAMS FOR ADULTS			
Enough	—	—	35
Not enough	—	—	64
Too many	—	—	2
			(1772)
EDUCATIONAL PROGRAMS FOR CHILDREN			
Enough	—	—	35
Not enough	—	—	64
Too many	—	—	2
			(1771)
INFORMATION ABOUT NATIONAL PROBLEMS			
Enough	—	—	58
Not enough	—	—	37
Too many	—	—	5
			(1823)

television—movies with social messages, "nature shows like *Wild Kingdom,*" and even programs that deal with problem areas such as divorce and premarital sex. Examples of educational programs in short supply for adults were much more likely to be drawn from commerical TV. *60 Minutes* led the list, followed by National Geographic Specials, Jacques Cousteau Specials, *20/20,* and PTV's *Nova.* But again the range was broad, with examples taken from straight news programs, documentaries, movie classics, and even game shows.

It also appears that the other question which drew a majority of "not enough" answers (in 1970 and 1980)—programs that offer advice or help solve problems—evoked a fairly wide range of interpretation. When asked to give examples there were a number of mentions of Phil Donohue, some, again, of *60 Minutes,* several of specific consumer protection offerings, usually presented as part of the local news, and a scattering of programs dealing with such topics as medicine, cooking, body building, and fishing. Though there was wide variation, the choices for emulation generally came from programming areas that would normally be classified as education or information, rather than entertainment.

The desire to be informed by viewing televison is found also in the answers to two other questions that were used in all three surveys. Steiner phrased, and we replicated, an attempt to compose two very broad sorts of content—"more informational content" versus "the best entertainment possible" (table 4.8). In the 1960 and 1970 surveys "best entertainment" beat out "more information" by a fairly convincing margin. In 1980, the two were virtually tied at about a third, with the remaining third of the popu-

Table 4.8
"Generally speaking would you say that television should provide more informational material or should it concentrate on providing the best entertainment possible?"

Percent Who Say:	1960	1970	1980
Provide more informational material	31	24	32
Provide best entertainment	40	38	34
Both, can't choose, don't know	29	38	34
Base: 100% =	(2335)	(1843)	(2002)

Table 4.9
"What are some of your favorite programs—those you watch regularly or whenever you get a chance?"

Favorite Program Types	Grade School 1960	Grade School 1980	High School 1960	High School 1980	College 1960	College 1980	TOTALS 1960	TOTALS 1980
Light entertainment	87	76	87	72	66	59	83	68
News, information and public affairs	8	15	9	18	22	33	12	23
Base: 100% =	(627)	(235)	(1214)	(1118)	(516)	(708)	(2357)	(2061)

lation wanting both. The second question provides more for a report on behavior than a pure assessment of attitude (table 4.9). Here we see, in the totals for 1960 and 1980, a doubling in the proportion that chooses a "favorite" program from the selections offered in the general category of "news, information, and public affairs." During the same period, the programs in that category as a proportion of the total TV fare also doubled. The differences among the educational groups are rather as ecxpected. In both 1960 and 1980 the better educated—particulary those with some college—are more apt to choose informational programs as their favorites.

Commercials

The American public has always had mixed feelings about advertising in the mass media. As long ago as 1949, George Gallup asked his respondents in a national survey whether they thought "advertising adds to or takes away from your interest" in the various media. It was too early in the game for television, but 44 percent of radio listeners said it "adds to" the interest, with 38 percent saying it "takes away." The rest had no opinion or thought it made no difference. A 1974 comparison of attitudes toward advertising on television with the ads in other media was provided by a study conducted for the American Association of Advertising Agencies. Among the people who generally liked ads, TV's products were rated lower than those on radio and the ones in newspapers and maga-zines, but higher than the ones they saw on billboards and in direct mail. As for TV ads themselves, about 60 percent of the public had favorable overall opinions and 40 percent unfavorable (Bartos and Dunn, 1976). In a more recent national study by the Roper organi-zation, 60 percent of the population said "most" or "some" in answers to the questions "How much television advertising is useful and informative?" (The Roper Organization, 1979.)

Gary Steiner found the public similarly divided about advertising on television in the 1960 survey (table 4.10). A majority thought that most commercials were too long, but a majority also found "some commercials are very helpful in keeping me informed." Forty percent agreed that "commercials are generally in poor taste and very annoying," but 36 percent agreed that "some commercials are so good that they are more entertaining than the programs" and three-quarters of the viewers found commercials to be "a fair price to pay for the programs you get." Certainly this does not add

Table 4.10
"Here are some statements about commercials. I'd like you to read each statement and mark whether you generally agree or disagree with each statement."

Percent Who Agree That:	1960	1970	1980
Commercials are a fair price to pay for the entertainment you get	75	70	62
Most commercials are too long	63	65	67
I find some commercials very helpful in keeping me informed	58	54	48
Some commercials are so good that they are more entertaining than the program	43	54	48
I would prefer TV without commercials	43	48	57
Commercials are generally in poor taste and very annoying	40	43	49
I frequently find myself welcoming a commercial break	36	35	36
I'd rather pay a small amount yearly to have TV without commercials	24	30	42
There are just too many commercials	Not Included in 1960	70	75
Base: 100% =	(2427)	(1900)	(2078)

up to the sort of overwhelming enthusiasm the 1960 population showed for television in general, but neither was it a broad indictment.

Over the past twenty years the public became somewhat more critical of commercials; more thought them too long, more expressed a preference for TV without commercials, and more thought them to be in poor taste. The proportion of respondents finding "some commercials very helpful in keeping me informed" decreased during the twenty-year period from 58 percent to 48 percent.

The proportions in our surveys agreeing that commercials are "a fair price to pay" for television fell from 75 percent to 62 percent. This less favorable attitude toward commercials is in the same direction, if not as sharp, as the decine in regard for television generally, and may it be a component of that more general attitude decline. Note that the two items that offered a *comparison* with the rest of TV changed hardly at all from 1960 to 1980. The proportion saying that they welcomed a commercial break remained just the same; the proportion finding some commercials so good "that they are more entertaining than the program" actually increased slightly from 43 to 48 percent. Other research has also found that commercials have fared surprisingly well in recent years when compared with other elements in television broadcasting. The Roper polls, for example, asked survey questions from 1976 to 1981 on the "two or three things that most annoy people about television." "Too many commercials" declined as one of the choices from 50 percent to 34 percent; "commercials that are too loud" went from 31 percent to 23 percent. During the same period, "too much violence," "too much sex," and "programs that insult intelligence" significantly increased in their selection as annoyances (The Roper Organization 1981).

All three of our surveys asked questions about the features of commercials which people found objectionable. Steiner asked "What, if anything, do you dislike most about commercials?" With the advantage of the 1960 results from this rather broad question, we split it into two in 1970 and 1980, asking first, "Are there any products or types of things now advertised on TV that you think should not be advertised?" and "Aside from the things advertised, is there anything that goes on in commercials that you object to?" The answers to the question on products are found in table 4.11. In table 4.12 are shown the summarized criticisms of the style or method of presentation for all three years, using throughout the categories developed by Steiner for coding the 1960 results.

In the second two surveys, about half the respondents gave some examples of objectionable products. This may have happened in 1960 also, but Steiner's questionnaires are not available for recoding on that dimension, so we cannot tell beyond the hint that drugs, medicines, soaps, cleaners, and tobacco were frequent

Table 4.11
"Are there any products or types of things now advertised on TV that you think should not be advertised on television?" "What are they?"

	1980				
Percent Who Mentioned:	Grade School	High School	College	1980 Total	1970 Total
Nothing, no, no answer	52	49	46	49	53
Cigarettes, tobacco	1	3	3	3	34
Liquor, beer, "booze"	10	11	11	11	16
Personal undergarments	6	6	7	6	6
Personal hygiene products	20	37	41	37	5
Drugs and medicine	3	6	6	6	5
Soaps and detergents	0	1	2	1	4
Products for children	—	2	5	3	—
Other	6	5	7	5	4
Base: 100% =	(235)	(1118)	(708)	(2061)	(2000)

Table 4.12
1960: "What, if anything do you dislike about commercials?"
1970; 1980: Aside from the things advertised, is there anything that goes on in commercials that you object to?" "What do you object to?"

Percent Who Mention:	1960	1970	1980
Nothing, no, no answer	53	61	64
Misleading, dishonest	16	8	8
Bad taste, suggestive	8	15	11
Stupid, unrealistic, silly	11	15	6
Boring, dull	17	1	1
Hard sell, aggressive	5	2	2
Base: 100% =	(2427)	(2000)	(2078)

1960 mentions. In 1970 tobacco and booze led the list of objectionable products. Even in 1980 a few oldtimers (3 percent) still mentioned tobacco products, even though cigarette advertising was banned from TV in 1971. The major 1980 enemy is the "personal hygiene" category, which includes deodorants and, above all, tampons. Objections to the advertisement of products in this category increased from 5 percent of the sample in 1970 to 37 percent in 1980. It accounted for more than half of the replies to the question in the later year, with the objections particularly strong among the better educated viewers.

The better educated also had a bit more to say about objectonable things that "go in commercials," aside from the products advertised, though relatively few of them, or of the less educated, had a great deal to say. Only about a third of the 1980 sample had comments to make on this question, compared with about two-fifths in 1970 and half in 1960 (table 4.12). Among those with comments, far fewer than before chose to criticize commercials as boring and dull. A number of respondents, though only half the proportion of 20 years ago, criticized ads for their exaggerations (coded as "misleading, dishonest"):

> The ads give exaggerated views of the effects of a product and what the product is supposed to correct.

> The lack of truth or "shaded" truth in some of the commercials—like dishwasher detergents that leave your dishes "virtually" spotless.

Some commercials were thought to be in bad taste:

> Washing the toilet bowl. They don't have to show this on TV.

> Sometimes the soap commercials show people in showers. I think this is a disgrace. What I think is disgusting in some commercials, they use sex to attract sales.

And some were still thought to be just too silly:

> When they bloat people up queer and say "in-di-ges-tion."

> The way panty hose is presented. Rather silly.

The way to keep a husband home for breakfast is to serve doughnuts.

A theme associated with many of the comments about objectionable features of ads, variously coded, is found in the statement of a college-educated respondent:

The men who are making them are super-sharp people, but I don't think I'm as stupid as the commercials try to make me feel. The men are super-sharp and the watchers are super-dull.

Despite such comments, the television commercial has not appeared to be a matter of overriding general concern to our samples. During the twenty-year period, the public has been split on questions of their objectionability and their utility, with the proportion having anything negative to say at all declining slightly.

Deciding About What To Watch

There are plenty of guides available—ads in the newspapers, daily listings, promotional announcements on television, *TV Guide*—but with all that it may be the viewer's own knowledge of the medium, and his viewing habits, that provide most of the guidance for program selection. In 1970 and again in 1980, when the respondents were presented with a list of possible ways to select programs, the most frequently adopted answer was "watch the same shows because you like them and know when they are on." About three-quarters of both samples say they "often" did that (table 4.13). The use of printed guides came in second, with a little over half of the respondents in both surveys giving that response. Watching shows picked by other family members came next, with about a third of the choices. Neither the rank-order of these methods nor the proportions saying they used each one changed significantly over the ten years. (Steiner had not asked the question in 1960.) We read these findings as meaning that most people, in their day-to-day viewing are so used to television and to its program choices, at least in mid-season when the interviews occurred, that they rely on their own

Table 4.13

"Now, would you please tell me something about what you do to decide on which TV programs to watch?" For example, do you often, occasionally, or practically never:

	Percent Saying "Often"	
	1970	1980
1. "Watch the same shows because you like them and know when they are on?"	76	72
2. "Make selections from TV Guide, or from the weekly guides in weekend newspapers?"	53	52
3. "Watch shows picked by other family members?"	35	31
4. "Read the listings each day in the newspaper?"	26	23
5. "Turn dial until you find something interesting?"	19	20
6. "Look up TV shows several days in advance?"	19	20
7. "Select from ads on the radio, in newspapers and magazines?"	16	18
8. "Watch one program and then just leave the set on?"	15	13
9. "Follow recommendations given children by their teachers?"	14	16
10. "Follow recommendations of friends?"	8	12
Base: 100 % =	(2000)	(2078)

acquired knowledge in deciding what to watch. There is a fair amount of consultation with some printed television guide, but much of the viewing public can often get along without it.

We searched in 1970 for a "selective" audience of people who relied on more than memory in deciding what to watch, and repeated the search in 1980. In both cases a multivariate analysis was performed using as the dependent variable a summary "planned viewing" score, composed of positive scores for selection of items involving the checking of printed sources (numbers 2, 4, 6, and 7 in table 4.13) and negative scores for dial twisting or just leaving the set on (5 and 8). In both analyses, our old friend education was the independent variable that explained most of the variance. The better-educated are more apt to check the outside sources. This can be illustrated by the answers to two of the individual items, as shown in table 4.14. The better educated check *TV Guide* or the newspapers more often than do the less educated; the less educated are more apt than others to just leave the set on, in both 1970 and 1980.

Table 4.14
Proportion Saying They Often:

	Education					
	College		High School		Grade School	
Item	1970	1980	1970	1980	1970	1980
Make selections from TV Guide, or the weekly guides in weekend newspapers	58	52	57	55	36	29
Watch one program and then just leave the set turned to the same station	7	7	15	16	24	18
Base: 100% =	(479)	(708)	(1017)	(1118)	(348)	(235)

Why People Watch

Even before the full development of the "uses and gratifications" approach to audience research, Steiner's questions on motivations for viewing were sometimes phrased so as to tap identifiable underlying needs that people were seeking to satisfy—to learn, to be sociable, to be entertained, to escape. Other suggested motives, as shown in table 4.15, appear to have been phrased simply to reflect common parlance, the normal ways in which people talk about why they do things—because I find it pleasant, because I feel like it. When the samples were asked how often each of 15 presumed reasons usually applied, the latter more commonplace reasons predominated (table 4.15). In each of the three surveys, the reason "To see a specific program I enjoy very much" led the list, possibly because it seemed so universally unexceptionable a reason for viewing. Other reasons may be a bit more discriminating. The second in frequenty in 1960, "Because it's a pleasant way to spend an evening," appears at least to be sensitive enough to reflect a trend. The drop of 20 percentage points between 1960 and 1980 in acceptance of that as a usual reason for viewing could very well be associated with the general decline in enthusiasm for television as a provider of entertainment, as noted in chapter 2. By 1980 it is no longer felt to be quite such a pleasant way to spend an evening.

A few of the changes in the selection of reasons for

Table 4.15 Reasons for Viewing

	Percent Saying Usually		
	1960	1970	1980
"To see specific program I enjoy very much."	80	81	74
"Because it's a pleasant way to spend an evening."	55	41	35
"To see a special program I've heard a lot about."	54	50	51
"Because I feel like watching television."	50	46	40
"Because I think I can learn something."	36	34	27
"Because my husband or wife is or seems to be interested."	21	20	16
"Because there is nothing else to do at the time."	20	27	25
"Turn on the set to keep me company when I'm alone."	20	24	23
"To get away from the ordinary cares and problems of the day."	18	21	19
"Mainly to be sociable when others are watching."	17	15	10
"Start on one show and then get stuck for the rest of the evening."	15	14	12
"Because I'm afraid I might be missing something good."	12	17	13
"Because everyone I know is and I want to be able to talk about it afterwards."	8	9	8
"Just for background while I'm doing something else."	7	10	10
"Keep watching to put off something else I should do."	2	6	5
Base: 100% =	(2427)	(1900)	(2078)

viewing over the 20 years suggest quite different lines of speculation. Two of the reasons that show significant decreases, for example, are viewing "to be sociable when others are watching," going from 17 percent to 10 percent, and because a spouse is interested, or "seems to be," 21 percent to 16 percent. During the same period, turning on the set "to keep me company while I'm alone" increases slightly, from 20 to 23 percent. These differences could very well be associated with a phenomenon that will be discussed in chapter 6—an increase over the years in the solitary viewing of television. Note also that only one of the fifteen reasons increased to a statistically significant degree ("because there is nothing else to do"), while most of them declined. Overall, far fewer reasons were chosen in 1980 than in 1960. Could it be that television watching has become such an ordinary activity, and is so taken for granted, that people no longer think about *reasons* for watching?

Why People Don't Watch

No direct questions were asked of the respondents in any of the three surveys about why they didn't watch *more* television, or why they weren't watching at times when they might have been. But with the use of the 1980 "last night" diaries—how each respondent was spending his time between 7 and 11 P.M.—one can get some idea of what the alternatives were. What was competing with television during the prime-time viewing hours? In the presentation of last night's activities in table 4.16, we show both the summarized activities of the total sample and, separately, those of the people, about a fourth of the sample, who reported watching no television during the four hours. Nearly half of the time of the total sample (48 percent) was spent with television. For another 22 percent of the total time, people were out of the house to work at a regular job, visit friends, dine, see a movie, attend a meeting, and so forth. If one adds to that the 12 percent of time spent sleeping, we are left with a total of only 18 percent of evening hours of the American adult public that is spent at home, awake, and not watching television.

　　The search for the available audience could perhaps be narrowed even further. If we assume that time spent at dinner in performing various chores around the house is not truly available for television viewing, we are left with only about 10 percent of

Table 4.16　Evening Activities 7:00–11:00 P.M. Distribution of Time

	Total Sample	Non-Viewers
Watching television	48	—
Out, at work	3	9
Out, dining, visiting, entertainment, etc.	19	42
At home, sleeping	12	17
At home, relaxing, radio, records, sewing, hobbies	9	18
At home, household chores (dishes, laundry, repairs, etc.)	4	6
At home, preparing, eating dinner	2	2
At home, personal chores	1	2
At home, doing other things or nothing	2	3
Base: 100% =	Approx. 8000 hrs.	Approx. 2000 hrs.

people's evening hours that could reasonably be devoted to television and is not. As suggested in chapter 2, we may be approaching saturation in the prime-time viewing hours. Of course, a variety of things do compete with television during that short period at home when sleep and household chores don't consume people's time—a bit of radio or phonograph, a game or two, a book to read, a sweater to wash. But all together these make up far less time than the other group of activities that take people out of the house and away from the set. A study of by John Robinson (which generally reports a much lower proportion of time watching television during a full week) also shows out-of-house activities as a major factor in decreased television viewing (Robinson 1977). During the evening, simply being at home would seem to be an excellent predictor of viewing.

The latter point is further demonstrated by a review of the activities of those members of the 1980 sample, in the second column, who watched *no* prime-time television. What were people up to if they watched no TV last night? They spend some of their time (more than the TV watchers) in miscellaneous activites at home, but the largest proportion of time is spent out of the house (51 percent). It is impossbile to say how much of this gadding about among our nonviewers is spent in the sort of leisure time activities that have traditionally been seen as competing with television for audiences (e.g., movies); nor is it possible to know the extent to which engaging in an extramural activity is a conscious choice between that and television. What does seem clear is that it is hard to avoid watching television unless one gets out of the house.

There is a related finding. In 1980, we also asked whether people who were watching television the night before were doing anything else at the same time. How much is television used as background noise while other things are going on? Our respondents reported that (27 percent) of the television-watching time also included some other activity—from gainful employment in jobs at home to trying to get to sleep (table 4.17). For 17 percent of the viewing time, television viewing was an accompaniment to household tasks like washing the dishes, doing the laundry, or repairing some piece of equipment. So indeed there is some overlap among

Table 4.17 Other Activities While Watching Television

	Percent of Time
Nothing	73
Doing household chores	17
Relaxing (sewing, hobbies, etc.)	4
Working at home	3
Eating, preparing dinner	1
Sleeping	1
Other activity	1
Base: 100% =	Approx. 3800 hrs.

the homely activities that might seem to be in competition for people's time—but only for about a quarter of that time—73 percent of the television time was spent watching exclusively or accompanied by activities not revealed to the interviewers.

Attitudes and Viewing Habits

In 1960 Steiner devised a scheme that permitted him to compare what the public said about television with what it watched. He obtained from American Research Bureau, the national rating service now known as Arbitron, a list of families in New York City who had completed diaries of the TV programs they had watched during a full week. An adult in these families was interviewed with a shortened vertion of the questionnaire used in the national study and the answers were matched with the diary records. The identical procedure was used in the 1970 replication, except that Minneapolis/ St. Paul was substituted for New York as the study site.

Steiner found relatively little relationship between such variables as age, sex, and education and what people actually watched. The better-educated, who said they wanted more "information" from television, did not watch very many more information programs than the less-educated. Neither background characteristics nor expressed attitude were good predictors of viewing. The 1970 findings were very similar. For example, when there was a choice between an entertainment program *(Marcus Welby)* and an information program *(60 Minutes),* shown at the same time, 65 percent of those with less than college chose *Marcus Welby,* but so did 58 percent of the college-educated. Of those who said they wanted better entertainment programs, 64 percent chose *Marcus Welby,* but so did 60 percent of those who said they wanted more information programs. Again neither the critical background characteristics, such as education, nor expressed preferences, proved to be very close related to what people chose to watch.

In the 1980 study, we used the diaries as the source of what people actually viewed. As noted before, when a respondent said he had been watching television during any of the half-hour periods between 7:00 and 11:00 P.M. on the night before the interview, he was asked to identify the program. We thus had over 2000 viewing accounts to use the analysis—limited, of course, to the prime-time hours of one evening. The viewing recorded in the diaries was coded into the program types used throughout the studies.

With the two previous studies as background, one should not be surprised by the 1980 findings, two examples of which are shown in tables 4.18 and 4.19. In table 4.18, which shows the complete television diets by program type for those who say that television should provide more information and for those who say it should concentrate on entertainment, we find at elast some relationship between expressed preferences and actual viewing, if only a modest one. Those who want more information do watch a slightly higher proportion of information and public affairs programs (16 percent to 13 percent). If we add regular news to the category, those who want more information out-view the others 28 percent to 20 percent.

Table 4.19 shows the distribution of viewing time for those with various answers to a question on learning something as a reason for watching TV. Again, the differences are quite small in choice of programs between those who do and do not consider learning to be a motive. One would expect the respondent's education to be a predictor of the amount of informational fare viewed, since the better-educated viewers have kept telling us they prefer programs that provide information over those that entertain. In

Table 4.18 Diet by Preference for Information versus Entertainment Programs (expressed in percentages of total hours of TV watched by program type)

	Those Who Say They Want:		
Program Type Watched	More Information	Best Entertainment	Both
Comedy-variety	20	28	22
Movies	20	27	26
Action	13	14	19
Sports	6	5	6
Light music	—	—	—
Light drama	11	14	12
News	12	7	10
Information and public affairs	16	13	14
Heavy drama	—	—	—
Religion	—	—	—
Heavy music	—	—	—
Base: 100% = (Approx. Viewer Hrs.)	(900)	(1300)	(950)

Table 4.19
"When you watch TV, how often does each of the following reasons apply?" Diet by Response to "I Watch Because I Think I Can Learn Something."

	Percent Who Say:			
Program Type Watched	Never	Rarely	Occasionally	Usually
Comedy-variety	19	34	22	22
Movies	18	16	20	15
Action	17	10	16	17
Sports	4	5	6	5
Light music	—	—	1	—
Light drama	18	11	12	15
News	14	10	9	9
Information and public affairs	10	13	14	17
Heavy drama	—	1	—	—
Religion	—	—	—	—
Heavy music	—	—	—	—
Base: 100% (Approx. Viewer Hrs.) =	(200)	(550)	(1300)	(900)

Table 4.20 News and Information Viewing as a Proportion of Total Viewing by Age and Education

	Age							
Education	18–29	(N)	30–50	(N)	51+	(N)	Totals	(N)
Grade school	22	(187.5)	15	(402)	23	(226)	19	(815.5)
High school	14	(229)	14	(563.5)	23	(369)	18	(1161.5)
College	24	(353)	23	(425)	28	(244)	24	(1022)
TOTALS	21	(769.5)	17	(1390.5)	24	(839)	21	(2999)

The numbers of cases are expressed in person-hours of viewing.

table 4.20 we show the viewing of programs classified as "news, information, and public affairs," as a proportion of total television viewing. Because of the relationship between education and age (older people are generally being less well educated), the table gives this nonentertainment viewing for each group within each education group. Table 4.20 shows that the choice of informational programs for the 1980 sample tends to be slightly bimodal for both variables. The youngest and the oldest of the three age groups watched a greater proportion of informational programs, as do the least and the best educated of the three educational groups. But it does appear that level of education remains only very modestly related to the type of programs that people actually watch, even when age is taken into account.

In all respects the 1960 findings are similar to those of 1960 and 1970. Neither education, the background characteristic that correlates most closely into program preferences, nor attitudes toward program types make very good predictors of what people will watch. Of course, one could counter by suggesting that how any people distribute their viewing time among different sorts of programs may be entirely a function of what is available to watch at various times; but what is not a completely satisfactory explanation. Even in 1960 Steiner found a much higher proportion of viewing time spent on news and information programs than the proportion of time devoted by the networks to such programs (people could choose such programs or other things available at the same time). Since then we have seen an increase in the number of commercial stations, the manufacture of better receivers, the introduction of cable into a quarter of the households and public television made reachable by 87 percent of the population. The Nielsen company data show that the median number of channels receivable in U.S. television households was about five in 1964, seven in 1972 and up to more than ten in 1981 when additional channels made available for some though the cable are included (Nielsen 1982.) People don't seem to be watching the types of programs they say they like nearly to the extent that they could.

An Audience of Opportunity

Some of the findings so far presented point to interesting conclusions about the nature of the general television audience. In chapter 3, it was noted that women watch more television than men, the older more than the younger, the less educated more than the better educated, and people living alone more than cohabiters; but if one equalized the opportunity by eliminating the normal work hours from the equation, a multivariate analysis showed no significant differences among such groups. Further (in the same chapter), an analysis of the previous night's viewing showed very similar amount of viewing among various subgroups in the population, when they were at home. Mere opportunity seemed to be the chief controlling factor in the *amount* someone watched. In this chapter we have seen how little difference either the most important background characteristic of the viewers or their expressed views about TV content made in determining what *sorts* of programs people will watch. This is not to say that people fail to make choices of programs among those that are available during their TV viewing time; of course they choose. But their viewing does not seem to be so motivated by their predispositions and preferences that they will either stay glued to the sorts of fare they say they want (whether information or entertainment) or turn off the set if they can't get what they would prefer. It appears as though factors other than predispositions and expressed preferences are affecting program choices, just as something other than personal characteristics and related attitudes are affecting how much people will watch.

These conclusions suggest a hypothesis that has been expressed before in audience research, in various fashions. There is, for instance, the ancient study by Bernard Berelson on "What Missing the Newspaper Means," occasioned by the 1945 newspaper strike in New York City (Berelson 1949). Berelson found that what many people missed was something to hold as they rode to work on the subway, something to thumb through and glance at so as to know what's going on—in short something to engage their casual attention, rather than to confront their intellects or stimulate their partisan fervor. The demand was modest but the *need* was deeply felt; in fact, Berelson refers to newspaper reading in New York in 1945 as a "ceremonial or ritualistic or near-compulsive act" for many people. For those people the act of reading was more important than what they read.

A parallel conception appeared much later in reference to the television audience in England. Andrew Ehrenberg and his colleagues have developed what they call the "duplication of viewing law." The law states, in effect, that the audience for any new program depends primarily on the number of people available to watch during the time when it's broadcast, and that can be discovered by seeing who watched some previously broadcast program in the same time slot. Who wants to see what doesn't count for much.

The American communication researcher Leo Bogart has another conception. He refers to some television viewing as a "pastime," meaning something done without much conscious purpose—perhaps like humming a tune or daydreaming. Bogart questions the assiduous quest for the "reasons" that people watch so much (as pursued by many audience researchers), since he doesn't see much motive behind much viewing (Bogart 1958). "Pastime" may be too lackadaisical a term, but still as far as an explanation for amount or content of viewing, our data do not suggest much in the way of strong motivation to view more television or less television, or any very careful attention to program selection for preferred content.

CHAPTER FIVE
Television News

L ate winter of 1960, when the interviewing for the first study in the series was carried out, was a "normal" time, a time, says Steiner, of "no national elections or conventions; no wars or police actions started or ended; no McCarthy or Kefauver hearings and no space flights. The major special coverage of the season was the Winter Olympics," and there was "no major technical innovation in the medium itself." It was indeed a good period to conduct a baseline study of attitudes toward the medium, if one wished to minimize the influences on those attitudes produced by such matters as the transmission of exciting or alarming news or the introduction of interesting technical features, and to concentrate on views about the content generated by the medium's own producers (with a 1960 content designed primarily to entertain).

If the 1960 study followed a "normal" period, the events leading up to the 1970 study were certainly abnormal. During the preceding decade the expanding TV news coverage had brought the on-camera assassination of President Kennedy and the subsequent killing of Lee Harvey Oswald, the space flights and landings on the moon, the Vietnam war and the violence and heroism of the civil rights movement. The bitter and hard-fought Nixon-Humphrey presidential election had culminated in Nixon's narrow victory about 15 months before the interviewing. On the technical side, the sixties saw the introduction and widespread adoption of color TV and the use of satellites in global transmissions. Thus the two sorts of exogenous influence that could affect attitudes toward the medium as a news transmitter must have been at their strongest.

In that respect, 1980 was an in-between year. Vietnam was over; we had the Iranian crisis, but not quite so intimately covered by television after our camera crews were expelled. There was no presidential election, with the 1980 campaign not yet underway and the 1976 Carter-Ford race dim in memory. The most widely adopted technical innovation was cable, which reached a quarter of the households but had little effect on viewing habits. Video cassettes and related technology were matters for the future except among a tiny proportion of the population.

During the two decades the content of television also changed in a manner reflective both of the shifting nature of events in the external world and of the medium's technical capacity to cover them. The proportion of total broadcasting time devoted to news, information and public affairs increased from 13 percent in 1960 to 24 percent in 1970, while total programming was also increasing, (see table 2.1). Over the following ten years, the proportion continued to increase but at a much slower rate, going from 24 percent to 27 percent. Similarly the public's reaction to television as a journalistic medium appears to have paralleled the changes in content (see table 2.4). Between 1960 and 1970 there was a marked increase in the proportions of the population that chose television over the other mass media as the one with "the most complete news coverage" (19 percent to 41 percent), which "brings the news most quickly" (36 percent to 54 percent), which "presents the fairest news" (29 percent to 33 percent) and which gives the "clearest understanding of candidates and issues in national elections" (42 percent to 59 percent). The average percent increase in those saying "television" on these four items was 15 points. Between 1970 and 1980 the proportions saying television continued to increase, but only by an average of five percentage points. The Roper organization, which has conducted surveys on public uses of the mass media and attitudes toward them since 1959, has produced similar findings. Television has superseded radio, newspapers, and magazines as the source of the most news "about what's going on in the world today," and the medium that people are "most inclined to believe" in case of conflict. The percentage change on both questions was more than twice as large during the period 1961 to 1971 as during the period 1971 to 1980. (The Roper Organization 1981.)

The continuing but somewhat tempered advance of television as the predominant news medium is also indicated in the answers to two questions discussed in the previous chapter. The 1970 sample pointed to journalistic features as the major changes that had taken place during the previous decade. In 1980 television journalism was still noted as a positive change of the 1970s, but not as frequently. Also, in answering questions about the "biggest moment" on television, the 1970 respondents mainly mentioned things covered by the news cameras. In 1980 news was jointed by a sprinkling of documentaries and sports features.

Though slowing, the trend continues, and the switch to television has taken place among all subgroups in the population. For example, in table 5.1 we can see the changes in assessment between 1960 and 1980 of four mass media—radio, newspapers,

Table 5.1
"Which of the media (radio, newspapers, television, magazines):"

	Education					
	Grade School		High School		College	
	1960 %	1980 %	1960 %	1980 %	1960 %	1980 %
Gives the most complete news coverage?						
Television	26	59	18	55	10	42
Newspapers	48	22	62	29	69	41
Radio	24	16	15	10	12	7
Magazines	1	1	1	3	1	10
Gives the closest understanding of candidates and issues in elections?						
Television	50	69	44	63	30	40
Newspapers	30	9	39	20	40	28
Radio	7	5	5	2	2	2
Magazines	2	2	6	6	25	21
Brings the latest news most quickly?						
Television	42	70	36	64	30	60
Newspapers	5	5	4	4	5	7
Radio	51	24	58	29	63	32
Magazines	—	—	—	1	—	—
Presents things most intelligently?						
Television	37	65	26	50	13	27
Newspapers	28	11	36	25	39	32
Radio	11	8	8	5	7	7
Magazines	18	9	27	14	36	28
Base: 100% =	(627)	(235)	(1214)	(1118)	(516)	(708)

television, and magazines—among three educational groups. Though the better educated show less appreciation than others of television as a new medium in both 1960 and 1980, they participated in the trend. The proportion of the college educated to choose television as the medium that brings the news quickly and presents it most intelligently doubled during the two decades; for understanding of campaigns, the proportion of those choosing TV increased by a third, and the proportion of those saying its coverage was the most complete quadrupled.

Journalistic Bias

The American public tends to be a bit suspicious of the objectivity of news reports, no matter what the source (Jacobsen 1969). Televison news comes off comparatively well. By 1980, 36 percent of our total sample picked TV as the least biassed of the media, up from 29 percent in 1960 (see table 2.4). During the same period, newspapers slid from 31 percent "least biassed" to 20 percent. The emergence of television as a news medium naturally brought it under attack from those who objected to some of its portrayals of events in which they were intimately involved. At the time of the 1970 survey the widely publicized speech of Vice President Spiro Agnew, in November 1969, was still in the public's mind. The Vice President had accused television of bias against President Nixon's policies. Much more recently, after our interviews were conducted, President Reagan was to blame the networks for a "downbeat" psychology in what he considered their overemphasis on the plights of the poor and unemployed. (*Washington Post,* March 18, 1982.) Among the researchers, there has been only one whose work would have appeared to support the contention of anti-Republican bias. Edith Efron conducted a content analysis of network coverage of the 1968 presidential campaign. She concluded that her data showed a bias against Nixon in his race against Hubert Humphrey (Efron 1971). A reanalysis of some of Efron's data a few years later by some professional communication researchers, however, reached a quite different conclusion: "There is no evidence of any systematic bias for or against any candidate" (Stevenson, et al. 1973). For partisan bias, the case is unproved.

Our own data can add some information on what the public *feels* about the medium's intention or ability to bias the news. For that purpose a series of questions was added to the 1970 survey and repeated in 1980. One of our aims was to see if the viewer, given a fair amount of choice, would feel that he could find a presenter of the news who displayed reasonable objectivity in the way he gave his reports. We started by asking the respondents how they thought TV newscasters, *in general,* presented the news: did they give it straight or did they color it? Those who said the news was colored we refer to as the "critics." We followed with questions about the way the respondent's most-watched newscaster presented the news.

In answering the first question in the series, the majority in both years said they thought that TV reporters, in general, gave the news as it happened, with a slight increase in that proportion in 1980 (table 5.2). These findings were equally true for respondents who expressed different political orientations—liberal, conservative, or middle-of-the road. In each group a majority thought the news was given straight and in each case the percentage increased in 1980.

The next question, which identified the respondent's

Table 5.2
"Thinking of the people who report the news on TV, in general, do you feel that they let their own opinions color the way they give the news or do they report it as it happens?"

People Who Report the News on TV	Conservatives		Middle-of-the Roaders		Liberals		Total	Total
	1970	1980	1970	1980	1970	1980	1970	1980
Percent Saying They:								
Give it straight	53	58	56	62	53	59	54	60
Color the news	30	22	25	15	26	20	26	19
Mixed, some color it, some don't	10	11	12	14	12	12	11	12
Can't tell, don't know	7	9	7	10	9	10	9	10
Base: 100% =	(702)	(843)	(435)	(640)	(541)	(355)	(1678)	(1838)

own favorite newscaster (the one he watched more than any others) produced interesting changes over the decade (table 5.3). Among those who had a preference in 1970, most identified a network rather than a local newscaster (53 percent to 20 percent). CBS's Walter Cronkite and NBC's team of Chet Huntley and David Brinkley led the list. In 1980 there appeared to be fewer favorites to begin with— the "no one newscaster" answer going from 27 percent 37 percent— and when a most-watched one was identified he was equally as likely to be a local newscaster; network and local newscasters were tied at 32 percent each. The increase in news coverage at the local level over the decade, possibly aided by the death or retirement of some of the best-known network newscasters, seems to have dimmed the luster of network stars.

The question asked in table 5.2 about TV newscasters in general was repeated for the selected, most-watched, one (table 5.4). In the latter table we show separately the answers of those who saw some bias among newscasters in general—the "critics"—and those "others" who saw no such bias. From the totals in table 5.4

Table 5.3
"Is there any one particular newscaster you like to watch more than others?"

	1970	1980
Percent Who Say:		
Network newscaster	53	32
Local newscaster	20	32
No one newscaster	27	37

Table 5.4
"Do you feel that (Newscaster) lets his opinions color the way he gives the news, or does he generally report it as it happens?"

	Critics		Others		TOTAL	
	1970	1980	1970	1980	1970	1980
Percent who say chosen newscaster:						
Gives it as it happens	56	64	86	89	78	84
Colors the news	16	14	2	3	6	5
Mixed, some of each	23	22	7	7	11	10
Don't know, can't tell	4	1	5	2	5	1
Base: 100% =	(344)	(252)	(964)	(915)	(1308)	(1167)

we see that only 6 percent of the 1970 population who identified a most-watched newscaster thought that he colored the news; in 1980 this figure was 5 percent. Most people in both years (84 percent to 5 percent in 1980) thought that he gave it straight. Even among the critics, a majority said that the selected newscaster told it as it happened.

As one might expect, when some political leaning *was* suspected on the part of the favorite and most-viewed newscaster, it was usually in an agreeable direction from the standpoint of the sample member. We asked in 1980, as we had in 1970, about people's impressions of the tendencies of the newscaster—did he seem to be liberal or conservative or somewhere in between? Most of the 1980 sample said that they couldn't tell or found the newscaster in the "middle-of-the-road" category. When they did detect some direction, left or right, it was apt to be in the direction of the respondent's own self-proclaimed tendency (table 5.5). For self-identified liberals, 34 percent say he appeared to be liberal compared with 14 percent who say he appeared conservative. Similarly, conservatives felt that "their" newscasters appeared conservative. In the overall assessment, the public consistently fails to find the anti-Republican bias suggested by those quoted previously. In 1970, the total sample of viewers found the newscasters about equally oriented toward the left and right; 13 percent said "liberal," 14 percent "conservative" (Bower 1973). In 1980 it was 16 percent "liberal" and 25 percent "conservative," which suggests that more of the public actually sees a drift to the right in TV.

Table 5.5

"In the way in which [newscaster] presents the news does he/she give the impression of being liberal, conservative, or middle-of-the-road, or can't you tell?"

	Liberals	Conser-vatives	Middle-roaders	Total
Percent Saying Newscaster Appears:				
Liberal	34	12	10	16
Conservative	14	32	20	25
Middle-of-the-road and can't tell	52	55	70	60
Base: 100% =	(212)	(559)	(388)	(1159)

Such a modest shift should not divert our attention from the main findings. Television is increasingly seen as the least biassed of the mass media. By 1980 three-fifths of the public thought that newscasters in general gave the story straight and 84 percent thought "their" newscaster "tells it like it is." Where bias is suspected it seems to favor the conservatives slightly more than the liberals, but this is in line with a general shift toward political conservatism in the population at large; the proportions in our samples who identified themselves as conservatives rose from 36 percent in 1970 to 41 percent in 1980.

Political Effects

There are numerous ways in which television broadcasting has been shown to bear upon the political process in democracies. For instance, it has clearly affected the way in which politicians run for office, becoming probably the main element around which campaigns are organized (Mendelsohn and Crespi 1970). In that respect, it has affected the composition of campaign staffs and the deportment of candidates (if not their actual selection), and it has greatly increased the importance of campaign funds to pay for television advertising and prepare for television coverage. That, in itself, has become almost a campaign issue. Ex-Mayor John V. Lindsay of New York City reported to a congressional committee that "in my last race for public office, I was more likely to be asked about my success in raising money for television than how I stood on the issues" (NCCP *Newsletter*, 1972): Thomas Patterson, in an analysis of the media coverage of the 1976 presidential election, produces findings not unrelated to Lindsay's remark. He notes that all the mass media tend to put emphasis on the "game" of politics—the campaign strategies, including the raising of money for television coverage—at the expense of "substance," such as the issues and the qualifications of the candidates (Patterson 1980). He sees nothing distinctive in television in that respect; it just does it more. Patterson adds that television is more condensed and simplified in its treatment than the other media and that it pays more attention to the new issues created by candidates' goofs before the camera, such as President Ford's suggestion in his 1976 debate with Jimmy Carter that Poland was free of Soviet influence, and Carter's comment in the same campaign about "ethnic purity." Such dangers could render even more relevant the campaign staff's attention to the deportment and prior briefing of candidates before their appearances in front of the TV cameras.

On the potential voter's side, many studies have shown television viewing to be the major way in which people get information about candidates and issues in political campaigns. There is also an accumulation of evidence (e.g., McCombs and Shaw 1972) that television, by what it chooses to emphasize, helps to guide public perception of what issues are most important and what characteristics of candidates are most pertinent. This "agenda-setting" role of television, treated in several studies in the past several years, would, it is suggested, affect what people think they should be thinking about as they decide for whom to vote or whether to vote at all.

Such possible indirect effects of television on election outcomes seem rather firmly established, but when it comes to direct influence on voting, the best professional communication researchers find a clouded picture. Paul Lazarsfeld, in his precedent-setting study of the 1940 presidential election, found little in the way of conversion of political preferences, or voting, from one candidate to the other as a result of the mass media's coverage (Lazarsfeld et al. 1948). Rather, he found that people's predispositions guided what they paid attention to in the media and the media thus tended to reinforce their decisions to vote in the way they would have anyway. As to voter turnout at the polls, researchers noted in the mid-sixties that no increase in voting was apparent after television came on the scene, though the introduction of radio had been followed by a large jump in turnout (Campbell 1966; Glaser 1965). More recent studies have largely found a *moderate* effect of television on political behavior, at best. They continue to point to other significant influences and to factors that intervene between the viewing of political information and persuasive messages and actual voting decisions. The research in this area is well reviewed by George Comstock and his colleagues (Comstock et al. 1978).

With these general findings in mind we may look at the results of a few questions in our surveys on the public's perception of television's role in producing indirect or direct effects on their political behavior.

We have already seen that TV is rated considerably higher than newspapers, radio, and magazines as the medium that gives "the clearest understanding of candidates and issues in national elections." Standing by itself, without the comparisons with other media, television gets a generally positive rating though perhaps one not so resounding as the previous findings would suggest. Table 5.6 shows us that 54 percent of the 1980 public rates TV's performance in the early stages of the 1980 presidential campaign (some 10 months before the election) as "excellent" or "good," with 10 percent saying "poor." The comparable figures from the 1970 survey, in which the sample members were asked about the 1968 campaign, show a very similar distribution, with 57 percent saying excellent or good. That such ratings for campaign coverage are perhaps a bit low in comparison with the usual expressions of high regard for television journalism is demonstrated by the results of another question that was added to the 1980 survey, which we insert here for illustrative purposes. We asked "how good a job has TV

Table 5.6
1970: "Thinking back to the presidential election of 1968 for a moment—the one in which Hurbert Humphrey, George Wallace and Richard Nixon were candidates—in your opinion did television do an excellent, good, only fair or poor job in presenting the issues and candidate to the public."
1980: "Up to now, how good a job has TV been doing in presenting the issues and candidates for the 1980 elections: excellent, good, only fair or poor?"

	1970	1980
Excellent	13	9
Good	44	45
Only fair	25	26
Poor	8	10
Don't know	10	10
Total (N)	(1856)	(2051)

been doing in covering what is going on in Iran," with the same answer categories of excellent, good, only fair, and poor (table 5.7). The coverage was rated excellent or good by 80 percent of the sample, with only 6 percent saying poor.

Of course, there was a general national consensus of opposition to what had happened to our Teheran Embassy and its staff, shared by television commentators and the public alike, whereas in any political campaign there is a distinct division among the public, pro or con, about any candidate covered. It is quite possible that some of the lower ratings for political coverage may reflect dissatisfaction with the coverage given to an opposing candidate, in a confusion of message and messenger that often occurs in media treatment of controversial events. This may be similar to a finding of the 1970 study, where it developed that the older viewers objected to TV coverage of the civil rights movement, apparently as much a result of opposition to the social disruption that the movement caused as of dissatisfaction with medium that portrayed it (Bower 1973).

Somewhat different approaches were used in 1970 and in 1980 to assess people's perceptions of TV's influences on their own political behavior. In 1970 it was felt that the interviewing was close enough to the previous presidential election, about 12 or 13 months, to ask a rather specific question about how television may have affected preferences in that election. In 1980, there was no such convenient reference point. The 1980 election campaign was hardly off the ground, and the previous presidential election was nearly four years old. A more general question was used, which is quoted along with the 1970 question in table 5.8. The marked

Table 5.7
"In your opinion, how good a job has TV been doing in covering what is going on in Iran: excellent, good, only fair, or poor?" (1980)

	Percent
Excellent	29
Good	51
Only fair	15
Poor	6
Total (N)	(2055)

Table 5.8

"Did TV play a very important part, a fairly important part or no part at all in helping you decide who you wanted to win in the election of 1968?" (1970)
"Do you feel that TV plays a very important part, a fairly important part, or no part at all in helping you decide whom to vote for in an election?" (1980)

| | Percent Saying Very Important or Fairly Important | | | |
| | 1970 | | 1980 | |
	%	(N)	%	(N)
Men	38	(974)	65	(883)
Women	47	(956)	60	(1192)
Young (18–29)	47	(410)	63	(597)
Middle aged (30–49)	44	(726)	66	(735)
Older (50+)	34	(699)	58	(732)
Grade school	40	(348)	51	(235)
High school	43	(1017)	61	(1118)
College	44	(475)	68	(708)
Liberals	43	(540)	69	(357)
Conservatives	44	(698)	62	(860)
Democrats	46	(915)	68	(959)
Republicans	41	(446)	65	(438)
Total Sample	43	(1830)	62	(2075)

increases in porportions feeling that TV plays a "very important" or a "fairly important" part, for the total samples, going from 43 percent to 62 percent, could well have resulted from the different historical contexts. In the more concrete instance of 1970, people may have noted the influence of other factors on any actual decisions made about candidates; in response to the more abstract question (1980) they may have had no reason to think of such influences and thought more about the general role of TV as a supplier of information about political matters. It could also be that the increased importance of TV in election coverage, as reflected in answers to the question about "which gives the clearest understanding," may have altered people's feelings about the influence of the medium on their own behavior.

In respect to intrasample differences, what seemed remarkable in 1970 appears again in 1980. The differences among the sample components are quite small, and where they exist they tend not to be in line with expectations. First, we see that slightly more women than men in 1980 feel some influences of television on voting—a reversal of 1970, when somewhat more men saw an influence on political choices. More interesting are the distributions by education. Given the better-educated viewers' usual skepticism about the virtues of the medium, one might expect them to display more immunity to its influence. But not so. In 1980, 68 percent of the college-educated felt that TV played a very important or fairly important part in their voting decisions, compared with 51 percent of those with a gradeschool education. Apparently a distinction must be made between the *affect* involved in people's attitudes— think well of it, think poorly of it—and the cognition underlying an assessment of effect. Many of those college-educated respondents can dislike television in general and at the same time think it to be politically effective; in fact they may worry about it because of its political effects. The two places in table 5.8 where there is remarkably *little* difference are in respect to the respondent's political preferences, with Republicans and Democrats seeing a rather similar effect, and in respect to political philosophy, with fairly similar proportions of liberals and conservatives seeing an effect.

These last findings help to answer one of the questions raised in this chapter—does the public's use of television as the chief source of information about politics help one party or political position over another, so as to affect outcomes? A considerable proportion of the public felt that it was aided in making political decisions by television, both in the specific instance of the 1968 election and in the early stages of the 1980 campaign. But TV's perceived influence seems, in both cases, to have been very evenly spread along the political spectrum. Added to that is the finding that bias is detected by relatively few of the respondents and those who do detect it are as apt to come from one party as the other. All this appears to support the findings of previous research that television has, at most, a very modest effect on election outcomes.

That leaves us, however, with a further question to which our data do not provide an adequate answer. Does television really play the important part in helping people in their political choices that so many of them feel it does? The fact that one person's influence is cancelled by another's doesn't negate the influence. It does, however, fit well enough with theories about how other factors, for example selective attention to political content in line with predispositions, intervene between television and election outcomes. People are further influenced to vote the way their tendencies were already directing them. It is our guess, as suggested before, that many of our respondents who feel the influence are not making the sharp distinction that political scientists, or other phrasers of questions in surveys, would have liked between television the informer and television the persuader. Any actual persuasion that occurs may well come as a secondary effect of the information, interpreted and used to reinforce predispositions.

The other main finding of this chapter hardly needs interpretation. In 1970 a strong trend toward television as the primary source of news was observed. In 1980, the trend was seen to continue at a slower pace. By that date, television was chosen above newspapers, magazines, and radio as the medium that gave the most complete coverage, brought the news most quickly, presented the least biassed news, and gave the clearest understanding of candidates and issues in elections.

CHAPTER SIX

Television in the Family

M uch of the early speculation about television con
cerned its potential effects on the American fam-
ily, an institution already battered by the automobile (which had
taken young people away from home and changed the rituals of
courtship), and by the various worksaving devices that rendered
children's help less essential around the house. It was thought that
television could bring the family together again—at least to the
extent of assembling its members in one room from time to time.
Steiner, though he was not directly concerned with questions of
family integration, did listen to what his respondents had to say.
For instance, in answer to a very open-ended question, "How do
you feel about television in general?", he noted that many more
thought it "helped bring the family together" than thought it "in-
terfered with family life," though most answered the question in
quite different terms.

By 1970 TV sets had invaded almost all American homes
and a third of the households had more than one set in working
order—a proportion that reached 60 percent by 1980. That phenomenon added another question to the inquiry: Do those extra sets
mean that once more family members go their separate ways? In
1970, and again in 1980, we attempted to answer the question by
asking about each set in the house—where was it, when was it apt
to be turned on, who watched it?

Viewing Together

To set the scene, a question in the 1970 and 1980 surveys asked the
location of each working TV receiver in the household. In both years
most of the respondents in single-set households had put the set in
the livingroom (76 percent in 1970, 70 percent in 1980). Most-used
sets in multiset households were also usually found in livingrooms

(63 percent in both surveys), followed by the "family" room (about a fourth in both surveys). Also, as shown in table 6.1, the distribution of the extra sets remained about the same, mainly going into one or another bedroom. What really enhanced the opportunity for household members to view by themselves was the increase in the proportion of households having two or more sets, in our samples from 42 to 59 percent. For the nation as a whole, another purely demographic factor has added to that opportunity. According to U.S. Census data, the proportion of single-person households in the U.S. increased from 17 percent in 1970 to 23 percent in 1980, an increase of about a third. Data from our own surveys on single-set households show that the likelihood of joint viewing around that one TV set decreased from 86 percent in 1970 to 76 percent in 1980, probably explained largely by the national increase of single-person households (not shown in table form).

To examine the changing patterns of viewing with others in situations free from such demographic trends, we can now concentrate on *families* here defined as a husband and wife living together with at least one child at home. Table 6.2 shows the proportion of sets around which there is said to be joint viewing in such families. In both 1970 and 1980 the likelihood of joint television

Table 6.1 Distribution of Sets in Single and Multiset Households, 1970 and 1980.

	The Only Set in One-Set Households		The Main Set in Multiset Households		The Additional Sets in Multiset Households	
	1970	1980	1970	1980	1970	1980
Livingroom	76	70	63	63	7	5
Family room	16	19	22	26	11	7
Bedroom(s)	4	8	10	6	62	69
Recreation or play room	1	1	2	3	10	7
Kitchen	1	1	3	2	6	9
Dining room	1	1	1	1	2	1
Other room	—	—	—	—	2	2
No special location (portable)	—	—	—	—	1	1
Base (No. Sets): 100% =	(1036)	(812)	(738)	(1214)	(952)	(1773)
N (No. of households) =	(1036)	(812)	(738)	(1214)	(738)	(1214)

Table 6.2 Joint Viewing in One-Set and Multiset Families

	Joint Viewing Likely			
	1970		1980	
	%	(N)	%	(N)
One-set families	94	(472)	93	(220)
Two-set families	80	(543)	75	(532)
Three-set families	66	(160)	69	(246)
Four-set families	65	(35)	63	(174)
Total for all sets	83	(1210)	75	(1172)

Table 6.3 Viewing Combinations in Single-Set and Multiset Families

	In One-Set Families		In Multiset Families[a]	
	1970	1980	1970	1980
Husband-wife	17	25	26	26
Entire family	55	41	34	36
Children	13	16	26	22
Mother-child	9	9	5	6
Father-child	4	8	7	5
Other	3	1	3	5
Base: 100% =	(443)	(185)	(613)	(597)

[a]Viewing around all sets, combined.

viewing decreases as the number of sets in the household increases. In 1980 joint viewing occurred 93 percent of the time in one-set families down to a still healthy 63 percent of the time among four-set families. With the increase in multiset households among the population at large, solitary viewing in families is on the increase, as shown in the totals which go from 83 percent to 75 percent for joint viewing. To turn it around, likely solitary viewing around the family sets has increased from 17 to 25 percent.

There have also been some slight changes since 1970 in the composition of the viewers that tend to get together in families when joint viewing does occur. Table 6.3 shows a decline in "entire family" viewing together in the one-set households and a somewhat increased likelihood that it will be the parents viewing together or the children viewing together. In multiset families, definitely the families of the future, the patterns appear not to have changed since 1970; the combined occasions of parents viewing together and children viewing together outnumber the occasions of joint family viewing.

Who Decides?

Although the future may bring changes, viewing still remains primarily a joint activity. The decisions on what to watch when family members get together are by and large mutual, if anything a bit more so in 1980 than in 1970. Table 6.4 shows the respondents' reports on decisionmaking in three situations—when a mother is watching television with one or more of her children, when husband and wife are viewing together, and when the entire family is watching. Mutual decisionmaking is reported more frequently in 1980 than in 1970 in the first and third of these circumstances, and also noticeable is the decrease in authority given to children. For example, when mothers and children are viewing together, children select the program 33 percent of the time in 1970, only 19 percent in 1980. There is a less pronounced diminution of the child's role when the whole family is watching together, from 17 to 10 percent. This shift is also noticeable among subgroups of the population. It was reported in the 1970 study, for instance, that children made the

Table 6.4
Who Usually Decides What Programs to Watch on the Set? (during particular time mentioned when more than one person watches it)

	Viewers					
	Mother and Children		Husband and Wife		Entire Family[a]	
Percent Who Report Decisions Made By	1970	1980	1970	1980	1970	1980
Group or mutual decision	27	37	53	52	42	53
Husband/father	—	—	28	28	27	32
Wife/mother	37	40	18	19	10	12
Child/children	33	19	—	—	17	10
Other, NA	3	3	1	2	4	3
Base: 100% =	(100)	(108)	(508)	(501)	(347)	(451)

decisions in 32 percent of the cases of black families viewing together (16 percent among white). In 1980 that proportion had
dropped to 15 percent. As we will see in a moment, the decline is
related to a general shift in attitude about children's TV viewing.

Perceived Effects on Children

Through the years the possible effect of television on children has
been the subject of more concern by parents, advocacy groups, and
governments than any other aspect of the pervasive medium. Israel,
for example, spent a considerable amount of time in a conscientious
debate in the Knesset before permitting television broadcasting in
the country. That debate was largely about the effect television
might have on national and social values in young, formative minds.
Communications researchers have also expended a great deal of
energy. An early work published in England examined a variety of
hypothesized effects of the new medium on children of various ages
(Himmelweit, Oppenheim, and Vince 1958) Himmelweit found no
clear overall answers about the benefits or detriments of television
for children in general. It depended on the child. For instance, she
found that television did affect children's attitudes and values on
such matters as social class differences, the characteristics of for-
eigners, and the roles of occupations; but only to the extent that
views were "not firmly fixed" to begin with. And gains in academic
knowledge, she found, occurred mainly among the younger and the
less intelligent children. Generally, the influences she did find were
moderate. Television was "neither distinct advantage nor severe
handicap" in school performance and its influence on societal values
was "not overpowering." A parallel work was published in the United
States a few years later, derived from studies conducted before the
results of Himmelweit's research were availaable. Wilbur Schramm's
classic *Television in the Lives of Our Children* came to quite
similar conclusions, though he was dealing with an American rather
than an English child audience (Schramm, Lyle, and Parker 1961).
Schramm also finds a rather moderate influence and he also em-

phasizes that the nature and force of the effect depends on what the child brings to the confrontation with the medium. In Schramm's words:

> It is not scientifically justifiable to say that television is good or bad for children. The relationship is always between a *kind* of television and a *kind* of child in a *kind* of situation. And always behind the child are other relationships of importance—notable with family and friends, school and church. Television enters into the *whole life* of the child, not merely the corner of it that happens to intersect a particular program.

In more recent years, American scientific research has concentrated on possible antisocial effects of television on children, especially its alleged potential for stimulating aggressive behavior, with many of the studies conducted under the guidance of the Surgeon General's Scientific Advisory Committee on Television and Human Behavior. In 1971 the Committee concluded—and the Surgeon General reported to Congress—that the research gave "a preliminary indication of a causal relation between television violence and aggressive behavior," operating on some children and in some environmental contexts (National Institute of Mental Health 1971). A decade later, the NIMH undertook a followup of the Surgeon General's report based on a review of some of the 2500 to 3000 books and articles that had been published in the interviewing years. The authors' report confirmed the relationship between TV violence and later aggressive behavior. On other scores, the conclusions were that "there is not yet adequate evidence to support some current beliefs that children have been led by lively television programming to be inattentive to material presented in the classroom," but that the evidence does support the opinion "that heavy television viewing tends to displace time required to practice reading, writing, and other school-learning skills." On television effect on physical and mental health, the committee found a dearth of research for drawing of any conclusions, and on certain possible pro-social effects, it was found that the research suggested that children (and to some degree adults) "can learn constructive social behavior, for example, helpfulness, cooperation, friendliness and imaginative play, especially if adults help them grasp the material or reinforce the program content" (National Institute of Mental Health 1982). Of course, other pro-social effects, such as the acquisition of useful information, have also been studied. All this work has been well summarized by George Comstock and his collegues, whose review again shows the disparity of opinion (Comstock et al. 1978).

A different type of summary has been provided in a paper prepared for the 1982 conference of the American Association for Public Opinion Research (Bygee, Robinson, and Turow 1982). The authors produced a useful modern estimate of TV's effects on children by contacting by mail some presumably knowledgeable professionals in communication research, asking them to give their views on the role of television in producing each of 18 hypothesized effects. The respondents were members of the Theory and Methodology Division of the Association for Education in Journalism and members of the Mass Communications Division of the Speech and Communications Association. Here is the list, as phrased by the authors, ordered from large effect to little effect in accordance with a scale that goes from "*The* cause" to "no relationship."

1. Increasing world knowledge
2. Enhancing buying behavior
3. Enhancing immediate gratification
4. Reinforcing social values
5. Increasing sex stereotyping
6. Decreasing reading
7. Decreasing attention span
8. Increasing curiousity
9. Increasing ethnic stereotyping
10. Increasing verbal ability
11. Decreasing creativity
12. Distorting political values
13. Increasing aggressive behavior
14. Decreasing physical activity
15. Increasing sex interest
16. Increasing alienation
17. Increasing pro-social behavior
18. Increasing verbal behavior

Among the topics that have been most studied, a "decrease in reading" comes fairly high on the experts' list of TV effects—number

6—and an "increase in aggressive behavior" rather low—number 13. Generally the experts appear to attribute rather modest effects to television, some positive and some negative. The experts with better qualifications (more scholarly publications) attribute *less* effect to television than do others.

Advantages and Disadvantages

What of our own sample of experts—the general adult population—including the parents of 1960, 1970, and 1980 who were asked several questions about how they thought television affected children? They certainly thought there were effects, and by and large they thought that the effects were benign (figure 6.1). In 1960, 70 percent of the sample felt that children were better off *with* than they would be *without* television. By 1970 that figure was up to 76 percent, possibly because of the appearance of *Sesame Street* during the sixties,

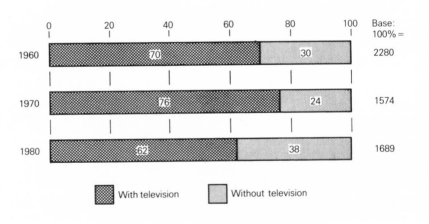

FIGURE 6.1. Percent Who Say Better Off
"There has been a lot of discussion about the possible effects of television on children. Taking everything into consideration, would you say that children are better off with television or better off without television?"

and in 1980 it had declined to 62 percent—in line with trends to be discussed later. In each case, parents in the samples were slightly more favorably disposed toward children's television than were childless adults. An adjunct to the "better-off" question asked parents who thought children to be better off with television to give examples of children who had actually benefited from the medium. Those who said "better-off without" were asked to give examples of harm. Table 6.5 shows the results.

Table 6.5
"Can you think of any actual example where some child you know or have heard about has benefited from television (asked of those who are pro-TV for children)?"
"Can you think of an actual example where some child you know or have heard of has been harmed or has done something harmful as a result of television (asked of those who are con-TV for children)?"

Percent Who:	1960 Parents	1970 Parents	1980 Parents
Give example of benefit (among those who say children are better off with TV)	34	43	34
Base: 100% =	(858)	(562)	(416)
Give example of harm (among those who say children are better off without TV)	24	12	41
Base: 100% =	(292)	(153)	(243)

A certain caution should be exercised in interpreting these data. The response to such open-ended questions, which require recollection from respondents, are particularly susceptible to the persistence of the interviewers, which can vary from survey to survey in an undetermined manner. Even with that disclaimer, it is interesting to note that the proportion of "better-off-with" parents giving examples goes up in 1970 and down in 1980, and the examples of harm given by the rest of the sample goes down in 1970 and up in 1980. These proportional shifts would tend to add some reliability to the up and down trends noted above.

Following the question on better off with or without, the respondents were asked what they thought were some of television's main advantages and disadvantages for children (tables 6.6

and 6.7). As may be seen in table 6.6, the advantages are perceived as largely educational—by 65 percent of the sample in 1960, 80 percent in 1970, and 76 percent in 1980 (up in 1970 possibly in response to public broadcasting offerings, and down again in 1980, in line with the results from the previous question). Another of the advantages, mentioned by 28 percent of the 1960 sample, was classified as "babysitting"—the use of television to keep children at home, occupied, and out of trouble. Such reported uses of television

Table 6.6
"What do you think are some of the main advantages of television for children?"

Percent Who Mention	1960	1970	1980
Education	65	80	76
Babysitting	28	16	12
Entertainment	19	22	18
Programs good generally	8	2	1
Stimulates socializing	1	2	4
"Adult supervision necessary"	6	2	—
Other, general	2	4	5
Base: 100% =	(2350)	(1592)	(1689)

Table 6.7
"What do you think are some of the main disadvantages of television for children?"

Percent Who Mention	1960	1970	1980
See things they shouldn't	51	52	48
Violence, horror	30	30	28
Crime, gangsters	10	8	9
Sex, suggestiveness, vulgarity	5	11	16
Smoking, drinking, dope	2	5	3
Adult themes	2	9	3
Harmful or sinful products advertised	1	1	—
Wrong values or moral codes	3	8	7
Other, general	8	2	2
Keeps them from doing things they should	36	30	29
Programs bad, general	10	2	2
Other, program content	4	6	11
Physical harm	5	5	1
Advertising too effective	1	2	2
Other	2	5	7
Base: 100% =	(2350)	(1583)	(1689)

have declined sharply, down to 12 percent in the 1980 sample. One suspects that there may be some new concerns about television that make it seem less attractive for such purposes.

When the same people were asked about disadvantages (table 6.7), about half of each sample mentioned some program content which they thought was bad for children to watch—they "see things they shouldn't." The sorts of programs regarded in this way, however, have changed a bit over the years. The content classified as "sex, suggestiveness, and vulgarity" increased from 5 percent in 1960 to 16 percent in 1980, while other themes, such as violence and crime, continued to draw similar proportions of mentions through the years.

We could probably assume from the sorts of advantages and disadvantages our respondents mentioned that some long-range outcomes for the children, good or bad, are in their minds, even if not explicitly stated. In 1970 we asked more directly about a few possible results of watching television with six questions—three rather specific and three very general. They were phrased so as to obtain a measure of how relevant people thought TV to be in producing the outcome, as indicated by the proportion who choose the opinion "TV watching doesn't make much difference" (see question wording in table 6.8), as well as to see whether people thought that television, if relevant, had a good or bad effect. Table 6.8 gives the results for both 1970 and 1980. By the "not much difference" criterion, television is not felt to be particulary relevant to the three more general outcomes—growing up in better health, getting into trouble, and becoming a "better all-around person." Among those who do see a television effect, there are more who find it deleterious than find it helpful, especially in 1980, and especially in respect to "getting into trouble."

Among the more specific effects, television is seen by our samples as having a definite positive role in teaching children about "what is going on in the world" and restrictive roles in the reading of books (those who "watch little TV" read more) and in doing well in school. The distribution of the answers to some of these questions was related to the eduation of the adult respondents. For example, 33 percent of those with a gradeschool education

Table 6.8

"Now, a few questions on the specific effects television might have in making some children act or behave differently from others: Who, do you think, are likely to do better in school, get in trouble, read more books, etc., children who watch a lot of television or children who watch very little; or do you think the amount of watching TV doesn't make much difference in how they do in school, how much trouble they get into, etc.?"

Which Children are More Likely:		Percent	
		1970	1980
To be better informed about what is going on in the world?	"Not much difference"	20	28
	"It depends"	11	11
	"Those who watch TV a lot"	63	48
	"Those who watch TV very little"	6	13
To read more books?	"Not much difference"	29	25
	"It depends"	6	3
	"Those who watch TV a lot"	10	7
	"Those who watch TV very little"	55	64
To do better in school?	"Not much difference"	30	26
	"It depends"	19	12
	"Those who watch TV a lot"	21	17
	"Those who watch TV very little"	30	45
To grow up as better all-around persons?	"Not much difference"	53	60
	"It depends"	11	4
	"Those who watch TV a lot"	19	14
	"Those who watch TV very little"	17	22
To grow up in better health?	"Not much difference"	53	55
	"It depends"	9	4
	"Those who watch TV a lot"	7	5
	"Those who watch TV very little"	32	37
To get into trouble?	"Not much difference"	58	47
	"It depends"	15	9
	"Those who watch TV a lot"	19	32
	"Those who watch TV very little"	9	12
Base: 100% =		(1900)[a]	(2078)[a]

[a] Less NA's, averaging about 8 percent.

thought that children who watched *very little* television would do better in school, compared with 48 percent of the college-educated. On who would read more books, 53 percent of the gradeschoolers said those who watched very little television, compared with 70 percent of the college-educated. Answers to the other questions were similarly related to education, but not nearly so strongly. On these items too, the effects are generally seen as less beneficial in 1980 than they were in 1970, consistent with the finding previously noted of a decline in the proportion of the population that thinks that children are "better off with" television.

Good and Bad Programs

The parents' choice of programs that they feel to be particularly good or particularly bad for their children would not necessarily represent the full range of views about television in general as being beneficial or harmful. There may be elements in any program that are thought to be informative and helpful, or vacuous and destructive, even though the whole program or series doesn't deserve such an evaluation. Nonetheless, the good and bad programs that parents have chosen in each of the surveys may provide some hints as to criteria for their evaluation. Tables 6.9 and 6.10 show the most frequent choices in response to the questions shown in the tables.

Most parents had a favorite or two in all the surveys. In 1960, the best regarded programs were, of course, all products of

Table 6.9
"Which of the programs your [child watches/children watch] do you think are the best programs for [him, her, them]?"

Most Frequently Mentioned					
1960		*1970*		*1980*	
Captain Kangaroo	19	Sesame Street	27	Sesame Street	39
Lassie	15	Walt Disney	21	Electric Company	12
Walt Disney	12	Lassie	10	Little House on	
Romper Room	10	Captain Kangaroo	9	Prairie	11
Father Knows Best	10	Wild Kingdom	7	Mr. Rogers	10
Huckleberry Hound	7	Jacques Cousteau	7	Walt Disney	8
Popeye	6	Romper Room	5	Captain Kangaroo	7
Dennis the Menace	6	National Geographic		Happy Days	7
		Specials	4	Eight is Enough	6
Base 100% = (1170)			(813)		(724)

Table 6.10

"Which of the programs your [child watches/children watch] aren't you too happy about?" (In Percent)

Most Frequently Mentioned					
1960		1970		1980	
Three Stooges	9	Dark Shadows	6	Three's Company	6
Untouchables	3	Laugh-In	5	Charlie's Angels	5
77 Sunset Strip	2	Three Stooges	4	Dukes of Hazard	4
Popeye	2	Mod Squad	3	Incredible Hulk	3
Base 100% = (1170)		(813)		(724)	

commercial television and were series produced for children. *Captain Kangaroo* led the list, followed by *Lassie, Walt Disney,* and *Romper Room.* By 1970, the most notable of the public television programs had taken over first place. *Sesame Street* led the list, edging out *Walt Disney* with other commercially shown programs making up the remainder of the top choices. In 1980, three out of the first five mentioned as good for children were public television offerings. From the standpoint of parents it was as if roles had been assigned—commercial TV for the adults and public TV for the children; but not without exceptions. *Little House on the Prairie* was still number 3, and Walt Disney was number 5.

The parents had far fewer nominations for bad programs for children, none of them from public television. In 1960, 9 percent of the respondents identified *The Three Stooges,* the pie-in-the-face slapstick comedy as the worst, followed by *The Untouchables,* about federal agents pursuing crooks with guns ablazing. In 1970, the *Three Stooges* had fallen to third place in a list led by *Dark Shadows,* a late-afternoon show designed as a spoof of horror films but not always so interpreted, and by *Laugh-In,* with its flicks of scantily dressed damsels. In 1980, we still have only a small proportion of the parents who can identify any particularly bad programs, but the composition of the choices suggests that violence and horror may have been joined by adult suggestiveness. The list was led by *Three's Company,* the comedy about a man living with two attractive girls, followed by *Charlie's Angels* with its three very modern girl detectives. To complete the list we have the *Dukes of Hazard* in which teenagers demolish cars in order to thwart the local corrupt police and the aging *Incredible Hulk,* with a some-times-bionic fellow throwing objects and people great distances. Violence remained as a feature of programs that parents disliked for their children, now joined by sex, although very few of the parents mention anything at all.

Parental Control

If, as we have seen, the children of 1980 were less likely than their counterparts of 1970 to decide what programs were to be watched— at least when they were watching television with their parents—we would expect to find a general increase in the controls that parents try to exercise over the children's viewing. As we can see in table 6.11, the proportion claiming to have "definite rules" about what and when their children watched did indeed increase, from 40 percent in 1960 to 50 percent in 1980, with the larger proportion of the jump coming between 1970 and 1980, corresponding to the decrease in the proportion of parents who thought that children were better off with television than without during that decade.

Table 6.12 shows the expected relationship between having rules and education; in each of the surveys we find more rules among the better-educated than among the less. As in other cases, the presistent relationship between education and the uses

Table 6.11
"Even though they're not always enforced 100 percent, are there any rules or regulations in your house about when and what your (child, children) watch, or do you let (him, her, them) make their own decisions?"

Percent of Parents Who Say:	1960	1970	1980
We have definite rules	40	43	50
We try, we make an effort	6	5	6
Children decide with minor exceptions	4	14	11
We have no rules; children decide	30	31	27
Don't need rules—children too young	7	6	6
No answer, rules not mentioned in response, etc.	12	2	1
Base: 100% =	(1170)	(813)	(724)

Table 6.12
"Even though they're not always enforced 100 percent, are there any rules or regulations in your house about when and what your (child, children) watch, or do you let (him, her, them) make their own decisions?"
Proportions of Parents with "definite rules," by parent's education.

	1960		1970		1980	
	%	(N)	%	(N)	%	(N)
Grade school	34	(230)	25	(84)	24	(26)
High school	40	(703)	43	(481)	46	(373)
College	47	(275)	46	(243)	58	(269)
Total	40	(1208)	43	(808)	50	(668)

made of television, by a population that itself is increasingly better-educated, can serve to explain some of the overall trend. If the 1960 attitudes of each educational group are projected to the number of cases in each group in 1980, the revised 1980 total would be 43 percent, an increase of three percentage points attributable to the demographic change. So almost one-third of the 1960–1980 trend can be accounted for by the change in educational level of the American population. The remaining seven percentage points over the two decades is likely to have been the result of an increased concern among all elements of the population, with the exception of those educated only at the gradeschool level, about the effects of television on children.

In 1970 we became a bit more specific about parents' attempts to control their children's viewing by adding some questions about individual children in the household. Parents were asked to identify all their children between four and twelve years old, and then one was selected at random for the questions shown in table 6.13. Consistent with the findings on "definite rules" discussed above, the table shows an increase between 1970 and 1980 of restrictions, both on times of viewing and on program content, in almost every instance. The most notable exceptions are program selections for the 10- and 12-year-olds, where there appears to be a slight decrease in the banning of programs in advance, some of which could be the result of the increased separate viewing by children in multiset households, as discussed earlier. We also see a decline in the use of television as a "babysitter," in encouraging the

Table 6.13

"Here are some things parents have told us they do with their children about TV. Taking just one of your children, do you or your (husband, wife) often, occasionally, or never:"

| | \multicolumn{6}{c}{Age of Child?} |
| | 4–6 yrs. | | 7–9 yrs. | | 10–12 yrs. | |
	1970	1980	1970	1980	1970	1980
RULES ABOUT VIEWING TIME						
Restrict Amount of Viewing						
Often	30	41	39	46	34	35
Occasionally	27	27	25	23	27	29
Never	43	32	36	32	34	36
Set Special Hours						
Often	41	49	48	58	46	50
Occasionally	26	28	18	26	22	25
Never	32	23	34	17	32	25
RULES ABOUT PROGRAM CONTENT						
Decide What Programs They Can Watch						
Often	45	50	37	46	46	40
Occasionally	28	30	25	42	38	29
Never	27	20	27	12	11	31
Change Channel When Program is Objectionable						
Often	40	51	27	60	30	52
Occasionally	30	27	36	29	40	28
Never	31	22	29	11	31	20
Forbid Watching of Certain Programs						
Often	39	48	39	51	52	45
Occasionally	27	25	29	30	22	36
Never	35	27	32	19	25	20
ENCOURAGEMENT OF VIEWING						
Encourage Child To Watch To Keep Him Occupied						
Often	18	12	13	8	7	5
Occasionally	32	38	29	38	23	16
Never	50	51	58	54	71	80
Encourage Child To Watch To Keep Him at Home						
Often	9	7	10	6	5	4
Occasionally	9	11	14	21	15	14
Never	82	82	76	74	80	82
Total (N)	(197)	(138)	(217)	(215)	(189)	(187)

child to watch to keep him at home or to "keep him occupied." This is in line with the findings noted previously.

This chapter has reviewed the major findings of our 1980 study as they compare with the results of the two prior surveys. Since we are limited to the views of parents and other adults, our results are not directly comparable with the results of most research on television's effect on children, which relies on inquiry among the children themselves, frequently following an experimental model. In fact, the relationship between the other research concentrations and what our adults think to be important is, at best, moderate. Throughout our series, parents have seen education as a major advantage of television for children, and indeed, scientific researchers have been studying TV's educational effects ever since the appearance of the classic Schramm and Himmelweit studies discussed above. On the other hand, the deluge of research during the 1970s on television's possible effect on aggressive behavior corresponds to no discernible shifts in parents' concern about the matter from 1960 to 1980, though it remains one of the worrisome factors when they talk about what may be harmful in the children's viewing. The actual *conclusions* of empirical research on children, with the constant finding of differences among different children when effects are seen to occur, may be reflected in some of our parents' views, as shown by the number who themselves volunteered the answer "it depends" when asked about television's specific effects. Generally our samples seem to agree with most researchers' conclusions that television viewing interferes with reading. They also feel that it detracts from performance in school, a question which the experts are still debating (Council for Basic Education 1982).

On other family matters, our data show an increase in the likelihood of separated TV viewing resulting from the extra sets coming into the households. Where more than one set appears, parents are more apt to view together, with the child or children viewing in some other place. That, along with the increase in the proportion of single-person households in the nation, has produced a trend toward *solitary* viewing, though viewing with others is still the norm, even in those households with as many as four operable TV sets.

Another change has occurred in some of those joint viewing arrangements. When viewing with parents, the children are less likely to select the programs to watch in 1980 than they were in 1970. This apparently corresponds with other findings, such as the *decrease*, since 1970, in the proportion of adults who think that children are better off with television than they would be without it, and the *increase* over the years in the proportion of parents who say they have rules which they try to enforce about the children's viewing. One of the rules, of course, involves the selection of programs. But perhaps that will become more difficult as the sets spread throughout the house and more of the children are viewing separately.

CHAPTER SEVEN

Constancy and Change

In the late fifties, when the Columbia Broadcasting System gave an unrestricted grant to the Bureau of Applied Social Research at Columbia University to conduct an "impartial nationwide study of what the public wants of television," no one imagined that the resulting survey would provide baseline data for a series of studies over twenty years. Instead of planning for a longitudinal analysis, Gary Steiner and his colleagues at the Bureau designed an elaborately thorough one-time investigation, employing all the techniques of the day. The questionnaire included both open-ended and structured questions, a variety of projection approaches, and alternative forms of the same question for administration to subsamples. The interviews lasted up to two hours and were carried out, with identical probability samples, by a two distinguished national field organizations, one commercial and one academic. The data reduction involved elaborate multicolumn coding schemes. By 1970, a complete repetition of such a study was out of the question: two-hour interviews were by then thought to be too burdensome on the interviewer and the interviewee, the coding procedures could not be reliably duplicated, and some of the approaches (like projective questioning) had simply gone out of style because of lack of confidence in their interpretation. In addition, the 1960 survey dealt in part with topics current in the late fifties, such as the quiz show scandals, and quite other matters became far more important during the subsequent decades.

So it would not be accurate to consider the 1970 and 1980 studies to be exact replications of Steiner's massive effort. We did, however, repeat a large number of Steiner's questions, in the same order and with the same wording, so that we would be subjecting our samples to common stimuli.

In this final chapter we can summarize the findings in respect to the two perspectives from which repeated studies may be examined. Surveys and experiments may be replicated for the purpose of confirming or denying findings, relationships, and hypotheses developed in the first edition. One searches for the *consistencies*. In our case, there are some relationships among the variables used by Steiner in his analysis that appear to be confirmed by the subsequent studies, such as a relationship between education and attitudes. In the second instance, we can look for the *trends*, the changes in behavior or attitude that have occurred over twenty years, in line with the original purpose for the 1970 and 1980 replications.

The Consistencies

Several basic findings remained essentially unchanged over the two decades. Education, which best seemed to separate those with favorable from those with less favorable attitudes toward television, was given some emphasis by Steiner in the first study. He noted the large differences between those with college education and those who stopped at the gradeschool level in the answers to question after question. The less educated like television better. With the techniques of multivariate analysis, which were available by the time of the 1970 study, it was possible to show that the relationship between education and attitudes held up even when the effect of other variables, such as sex, age, and income, were taken into account. This was demonstrated in reanalysis of the 1960 data and through analyses of the 1970 and 1980 findings. With three studies behind us, we are safe in the assertion that higher education decreases admiration for television as an institution.

Another strong predictor of attitudes toward television was all but ignored by Steiner in the 1960 study. Our multivariate analysis of Steiner's data, however, showed race vying with education in explaining the variance in attitude scores. Steiner, with his use of less advanced analytic techniques, may have missed this. Race continued through the 1970 and the 1980 studies as an important audience division. Blacks, even well-educated blacks, are more favorably disposed to the medium than are whites; they watch somewhat more overall and the college-educated blacks watch considerably more than their white counterparts. Very few black families have cable television—partly, but not entirely, because of geography and demographics. Our suggestion that the particular attraction of TV for blacks may be its use for vicarous participation in aspects of American society from which they have historically been excluded remains a hypothesis for testing in some future research.

With respect to age as a variable, Steiner found little consistency. In a few instances age seemed directly related to some other attitudinal or behavioral variable, but just as frequently it was bimodally related, with the old and the young showing something in common and the middle-aged off somewhere else. With the 1960 data as a baseline, we were able to carry out a longitudinal analysis of age cohorts to test the hypothesis of a continuity through the years of early-adopted views about television and the uses made of it, as opposed to changes in patterns as people grow older and meet new demands. The pseudo-cohort analysis of the answers to several questions, though the distribution of answers to the questions are not uniformly related to age, at least showed a pattern in 1960, 1960, and 1980 that strongly suggested it was the age-related demands of various stages of life that determined the attitude and uses of the medium, rather than a continuity of views that were formed early in life and persisted.

Another, seemingly peculiar, finding of Steiner in 1960 was the lack of relationship between expressed attitudes toward television and the public's actual patterns of viewing. Steiner's methodological *tour de force* was the comparison he was able to make of attitudes versus viewing by reinterviewing a sample of New York viewers who had completed diaries for the American Research Bureau (now Arbitron) of programs actually watched. What the sample members said about television appeared to be quite unrelated to how much they watched, what they watched, and what they chose when there was a realistic option, for example between an informational program and an entertainment program. It seemed peculiar because social scientists often seek and usually find a congruence between attitudes and behavior. Steiner's finding might have been set aside as another of those one-time flukes that appear in social research had we not had the opportunity to examine it twice more—in 1970 by replicating the 1960 procedures in Minneapolis/St. Paul and in 1980 by a "last-night's" viewing diary. It would not be accurate to say that in the two replications *no* relationship was found between what people said and what they did, but certainly it was a minuscule one.

By and large, Steiner's finding was confirmed. We found in 1980, for instance, that if one examined the amount of viewing in those hours when everybody was apt to be home, the better educated watched about the same amount as the less educated, and those who said they wanted information watched approximately the same fare as those who said they wanted entertainment. The one place where attitudes and behavior did correspond was in regard to public television—the better educated like it better and watch it more, though PTV is for all a rather minor diversion. Everywhere else attitudes proved to be poor predictors of viewing behavior.

The lack of a stonger relationship between expressed attitudes and patterns of viewing has led us to speculate, in chapter 4, about a television "audience of opportunity," following Bogart's idea of TV watching as a "pastime" not requiring much motivation, borrowing Berelson's finding from research on another medium of newspaper reading as "ritualistic," and adopting Ehrenberg's idea of sheer "availability" as a reason for the public watching what they do.

The Trends

There has been a clear and consistent increase in viewing from 1960 to 1980. By our measurements as well as those of the national rating services, the average viewing time has increased by about 27 percent. Our analysis shows that the increase occurred mainly in the first of the two decades and has occurred outside of the prime time evening hours, which seemed to have achieved close to the maximum audience by 1970. It came in the rest of the broadcasting hours—mornings, afternoons, late nights, and weekends. In the second two studies we concentrated our attention on the "equal opportunity audience" of viewers during the nonwork hours, after 6 P.M. on weekdays and on weekends. Here too we find some increase in viewing among all segments of the population.

Consistent with this increased viewing are the findings from the one question used in all three surveys, which asked the respondents to estimate how much they enjoyed the programs they actually watched. The proportion of programs found to be "very enjoyable" increased between 1960 and 1980 from 44 percent to 54 percent for the population at large. The proportion also increased for significant subgroups in the population such as those of different levels of education.

While that was going on, another trend became apparent. The appreciation of television as a *news* medium was growing, as discussed in chapter 5. Between 1960 and 1980, the proportion of the population that thought televison gave them the most complete news coverage had tripled, and in both 1970 and 1980 the increase in news coverage was seen as the most important change that had taken place in television during the previous decade. That was a rather accurate perception, since the proportion of broadcasting time spent on news and information did, in fact, more than double during the twenty years, either following the public appreciation for that part of broadcasting or leading it.

During the twenty years viewing increased, people enjoyed more of the programs they actually watched, and television was appreciated more and more as a journalistic medium; but still general attitudes toward television were declining. Our main measure of "attitudes toward television" has been the scale derived from seven "semantic differential" items, but the answers to several other questions, such as which of the media "is getting better all the time" or which of several things "are you most satisfied with," show the same downward trend. The public has drifted from high enthusiasm to modest appreciation for television in general. Some of this decline, perhaps a third, may be attributed to the increased education of the population at large, producing a higher proportion of those who would predictably have a less favorable attitudes toward the medium. Perhaps another factor has been a "novelty effect"— an early appreciation of the technological wonder, followed by a more thoughtful appraisal after the medium became a customary way of life. If survey researchers had been there at the beginning to study early and late attitudes toward the automobile, the refrigerator, or the airplane, a similar decline in enthusiasm might have been observed.

The tracing of changes on another topic—the attitudes of adults toward televison for children—does not reveal the smooth consistent pattern of increase or decrease that is found in the trends discussed above. In the question that asked whether children were thought to be better off with or without television, the proportion who said "better off with" went up from 70 percent to 76 percent during the first decade and then declined to 62 percent during the second. The appearance of *Sesame Street* may have been responsible for some of the increase in the sixties, but that excellent program was still around in the seventies and even better known by the public. The deline of the seventies appears to be associated, in the minds of the increasingly large minority who found children "better off without," with specific beliefs that televison impairs performance in school and discourages the reading of books. It may also be that some of our sample viewers were aware of the publicity given to studies of television's effect on aggressiveness among children, but the change most apparent in our samples' listing of television's disadvantages was the increase in those who found a danger in children's viewing of vulgar or suggestive content.

The Inconsistencies

Each of these trends can be partially explained to the extent that they need explanation at all; but what can be said of the apparent contradiction among them? How can the public be watching more television, enjoying more of what they watch, and think less of the medium in general? How can evaluations of TV journalism go up while attitudes decline? Unfortunately the studies themselves do not offer many clues to the answers, but one can speculate.

It may be that our questions on "attitudes toward television" tap rather broad overall feelings that are only partially related to the content of programs and that combine, as suggested above, a view of television as a technological innovation, especially in the early days, with an image of it as an institution producing good and bad effects for the world. Add to that the actual increase in programs available to the average viewer through more broadcasting channels and through the additional access to channels by cable TV, and it might seem almost reasonable that attitudes and enjoyment can head in opposite directions. Similarly, attitudes toward television and views about its provisions of news and information may be quite separable. It seems obvious that our attitude measures, to the extent they are related to specific content at all, tap views about TV as an entertainer, which is still where most of the medium's efforts are expended. The expansion of television's journalistic role is noted and appreciated when specific questions are asked, but it may not alter attitudes toward the institution, especially when much of the news is bad. With innovation effect declining, perhaps the rest of the television is not seen any longer as meriting such high praise.

APPENDIX A
Sampling Procedures

(As Prepared by The Roper Organization)

The sample for this study was designed to represent the adult population of the Continental United States, age 18 and over, exclusive of institutionalized segments of the population (Army camps, nursing homes, prisons, etc.). It was a multistage, stratified probability sample using an initial personal interview call and up to six additional calls in order to obtain interviews with designated respondents.

At the first selection stage, 100 counties were chosen at random proportional to population, after all the counties in the nation had been stratified by population size within geographic region. At the second stage, cities and towns within the sample counties were drawn at random proportional to population. Where block statistics were available, blocks were drawn within the cities and towns; where no block statistics were available, blocks or rural route segments were drawn at random.

Up to the point of drawing the block and route segments (clusters), the methodology employed is quite orthodox. From there on, however, the Roper Organization used a unique method of cluster selection, with the clusters divided into two matched groups of equal size. One set of clusters was designated as "daytime," the other as "nondaytime," an arrangement that evolved from a former Roper procedure of dividing interivew assignments into male and female blocks with different interviewing hours—mainly evenings and weekends for males, mainly daytime for females. Initial calls in daytime clusters were conducted during weekday hours, and in nondaytime clusters they were conducted in the evening (after 5:00 P.M.) or on weekends. Each of the 100 sampling points contain four clusters, two with assignments for daytime interviewing two for non-daytime weekend and evening calls.

In any particular cluster, the interviewer started at a designated house and called on the assigned houses in succession,

proceeding in a predetermined direction. The initial purpose was
to complete an enumeration of each assigned household, to be
accomplished by first determining that there were eligible respondents in the household and then by a listing of certain information
about all household members, whether eligible or not. Households
with eligible respondents are referred to as "information households." Interviewers, in order to complete their assignment, were
required to obtain 10 information households from each cluster,
from a maximum of 16 households assigned to each cluster. No
more than the 16 households were ever contacted, however, even if
10 information households had not been secured after the contacts.
The households where it was impossible to establish eligibility
because of no answer at the house, refusal, etc. are called "noninformation." Up to three calls were made at a household to get this
information.

In a daytime cluster an "eligible" is a person 18 years
of age or older who has no regular commitments that cause him or
her to be away from home more than one-half of the time between
9 to 5, Monday through Friday. Only people who do *not* have to be
away from home more than one-half the time during such weekday
hours are eligible for daytime interviews. If no one in the household
qualifies, no interview is made and the household constitutes a
"completed household" in terms of the interviewer's assigned number of households. If a person qualifies and is home at the time of
the initial call, the interview is made at that time. If a person is not
at home, up to three callbacks (in addition to those used to secure
household information) are made to secure an interview with that
person. If a household contains two or more eligibles, a random
selection pattern is employed to determine which one of them is
the person designated for an interview. If the person designated is
home, he or she is interviewed at that time. Otherwise, the three
callbacks are made to reach them. The interviewer may, in a household containing two or more eligibles, interview one other eligible
in the course to trying to interview the designated one, but no
callbacks are made to achieve this interview.

Nondaytime clusters are treated identically except the
definition of an eligible is the exact opposite of a daytime eligible.

The only people eligible for interviews in nondaytime clusters are people who *do* have commitments that keep them away from more than one-half of the time from 9 to 5, Monday through Friday. The same callback procedures are employed on nondaytime clusters as daytime clusters, though the call back is made at different hours and/or days of the week.

To summarize, any household contacted ends up falling into one of the following categories:

1. Households where eligible respondent(s) are identified and listed and interview(s) are made.
2. Households where eligible respondent(s) are identified and listed but no interview(s) are made.
3. Households where there is no eligible respondent(s), therefore no interview could be made.
4. Households where it is not possible to ascertain (due to refusal, no answer, etc.) definite information about the existence of eligible respondents.

Households in the first three categories are considered "information" households because information about eligible respondents (whether interviewed or not) is definitely determined. Category "4" households are termed "noninformation" because necessary information about eligibility of household members is not obtained.

1980 Questionnaire

Time started _____   Time finished_____   Total minutes_____   10-12/9

My name is _____. I'm from The Roper Organization, a public opinion research firm, and we're conducting
a study to find out how people feel about various things. All of the information that we gather will be treated
confidentially. This should take about 40 minutes--it varies depending on how much people have to say.

1. Here are some things that many people take for granted today. But imagine, if you can, that for two or three
    months you could have only one of these and you'd have to do without the rest. (HAND RESPONDENT CARD)

    a. If you could only have one of those things, which one would you choose?

	a. 1st choice	b. 2nd choice	c. 3rd choice	
Telephone...........................	1	1	1	
Refrigerator........................	2	2	2	
Automobile...............	3 ⎬(ASK b)	3 ⎬(ASK c)	3	
Television..........................	4	4	4	
Newspaper...........................	5	5	5	
Don't know..........................	8 (SKIP TO 2)	8 (SKIP TO 2)	8	13-15/9

    b. Suppose you could have two of them. What would be the second item you'd want? (RECORD ABOVE)

    c. And which would be the third? (RECORD ABOVE)

2. Here is another list of five different products and services designed to please the general public. (HAND
    RESPONDENT CARD)

    a. Which of these five things are you personally most satisfied with?

	a. Most satisfied with	b. Next best	
Fashions for women........	1	1	
Automobiles..............	2	2	
Television programs.......	3 ⎬(ASK b)	3	
Movies...................	4	4	
Popular music............	5	5	
None.....................	6 ⎬(SKIP TO 3)	6	
Don't know...............	8	8	16-17/9

    b. And which is next best, in your opinion? (RECORD ABOVE)

3. Now, I would like to get your opinions about how radio, newspapers, television and magazines compare. (HAND RESPONDENT CARD) Generally speaking, which of these would you say--

	Tele-vision	Maga-zines	News-papers	Radio	Don't know, none	
a. Is the most entertaining?........................	1	2	3	4	8	18/9
b. Gives the most complete news coverage?...........	1	2	3	4	8	19/9
c. Presents things most intelligently?..............	1	2	3	4	8	20/9
d. Is the most educational?.........................	1	2	3	4	8	21/9
e. Brings you the latest news most quickly?.........	1	2	3	4	8	22/9
f. Does the most for the public?....................	1	2	3	4	8	23/9
g. Seems to be getting worse all the time?..........	1	2	3	4	8	24/9
h. Presents the fairest, most unbiased news?........	1	2	3	4	8	25/9
i. Is the least important to you?...................	1	2	3	4	8	26/9
j. Creates the most interest in new things going on?	1	2	3	4	8	27/9
k. Does the least for the public?...................	1	2	3	4	8	28/9
l. Seems to be getting better all the time?.........	1	2	3	4	8	29/9
m. Gives you the clearest understanding of the candidates and issues in national elections?..	1	2	3	4	8	30/9

4. How many TV sets are there in your home that are in working order--including any that may be just temporarily out of order and waiting to be fixed?

_____ (ASK 5-10 FOR EACH SET)
(write in)

(SAY: "MOST OF THE REMAINING QUESTIONS ARE TO BE
None....... 0 ASKED OF PEOPLE WHO HAVE TELEVISIONS"--THEN
SKIP TO 74--PAGE 18)   31/9

	Set 1	Set 2	Set 3	Set 4
5. In what room is this set (the main set) usually located in the house? The other sets?	(write in)	(write in)	(write in)	(write in)
6. Is the set in (room) :				
Black and white...	1	1	1	1
OR				
Color TV?.........	2	2	2	2
7. Is the set in (room) hooked up to cable television (CATV) that you pay extra for each month or so?				
Yes..............	1	1	1	1
No...............	2	2	2	2
Don't know.......	8	8	8	8
8. Is there some particular time (more than any other time) when more than one person is likely to be watching the set in (room) ? (IF SO) When is that?	(write in when-- ASK 9)	(write in when-- ASK 9)	(write in when-- ASK 9)	(write in when-- ASK 9)
No time more than one viewer.......	1 (SKIP TO NEXT SET OR 11 IF NO OTHER SET)	1 (SKIP TO NEXT SET OR 11 IF NO OTHER SET)	1 (SKIP TO NEXT SET OR 11 IF NO OTHER SET)	1 (SKIP TO 11)
9. Who usually watches the (room) set during (time answered in 8 ?	(write in)	(write in)	(write in)	(write in)
10. Who usually decides what program to watch on the (room) set during (time answered in 9) ?	(write in)	(write in)	(write in)	(write in)

INSTRUCTION TO INTERVIEWER: TURN QUESTIONNAIRE TO QUESTION 11 AND HAND QUESTIONNAIRE TO RESPONDENT.
ASK QUESTIONS 11, 12 AND 13 FROM YOUR CARD WITH QUESTIONS 11, 12 AND 13.

11. Here are some "opposites." (HAND RESPONDENT RECORDING ON NEXT PAGE) Please read each pair quickly and put a check mark someplace between them, wherever you think it belongs to describe television. Just your offhand impression. (IF NECESSARY, EXPLAIN: For example, take that first pair--exciting or dull. If you think television is very exciting, you'd put a check all the way over here in the first space, or if you think it's pretty exciting, you'd put a check in the next space, or if you think it's very dull, you'd put your check all the way over in the right-hand space. Now, where would you put it to indicate how you feel about television?)

I just want your quick offhand reaction. Don't spend a lot of time worrying about it. (IF "SOME TV ONE WAY AND SOME THE OTHER," ASK: "How would you generally describe it?")

12. Now let's talk for a moment about reasons for watching television. Here is a list of possible reasons. When you watch TV, how often does each of these reasons apply to you? (HAND RESPONDENT PAGE 6 AND HAVE HIM CHECK ONE CATEGORY FOR EACH REASON.) For example, take "I watch to see a special program that I've heard a lot about." When you watch TV is that usually one of your reasons, occasionally a reason, rarely or never?

13. On an average day, during what hours do you yourself ordinarily watch television? (HAND RESPONDENT PAGE 7) Would you fill this out--just put check marks in each appropriate column--for a weekday, for Saturday, and for Sunday.

Please check each hour you would be likely to see at least some television. (DON'T COUNT TIMES WHEN SET IS ON BUT RESPONDENT IS NOT WATCHING AT ALL.)

11. Put a check (✓) between each pair--wherever you think it belongs--to describe television.

TELEVISION IS GENERALLY:

Exciting							Dull	32/9
In good taste							In bad taste	33/9
Important							Unimportant	34/9
Generally bad							Generally excellent	35/9
Lots of variety							All the same	36/9
Upsetting							Relaxing	37/9
Interesting							Uninteresting	38/9
Wonderful							Terrible	39/9
Nobody cares much							On everyone's mind	40/9
For me							Not for me	41/9
Too "simple minded"							Too "highbrow"	42/9
Getting worse							Getting better	43/9
Stays the same							Keeps changing	44/9
Informative							Not informative	45/9
Lots of fun							Not much fun	46/9
Serious							Playful	47/9
Imaginative							No imagination	48/9

12. When you watch TV, how often does each of these reasons apply?

	Usually	Occa-sionally	Rarely	Never	
I watch to see a special program that I've heard a lot about...............					49/9
I watch because there is nothing else to do at the time...............					50/9
I watch to get away from the ordinary cares and problems of the day........					51/9
I turn on the set just "to keep me company" when I'm alone..............					52/9
I watch because I think I can learn something............................					53/9
I watch because I'm afraid I might be missing something good............					54/9
I keep watching to put off doing something else I should do...........					55/9
I start watching because someone else in the house is watching and seems to be interested......................					56/9
I start on one show and then "get stuck" for the rest of the evening...					57/9
I watch because everyone I know is watching and I want to be able to talk about it afterwards.............					58/9
I watch just for "background" while I am doing something else............					59/9
I watch just because I feel like watching television..................					60/9
I watch mainly to be sociable when others are watching..................					61/9
I watch to see a specific program that I enjoy very much...............					62/9
I watch just because it is a pleasant way to spend an evening.............					63/9

13. Please check each hour you would be likely to see at least some television.

	An ordinary weekday	An ordinary Saturday	An ordinary Sunday				
6-7 A.M..............					64/9	65/9	66/9
7-8 A.M..............					67/9	68/9	69/9
8-9 A.M..............					70/9	71/9	72/9
9-10 A.M.............					73/9	74/9	75/9
10-11 A.M............					76/9	77/9	78/9
11 A.M. - 12 Noon....					79/9	80/9	81/9
12-1 P.M.............					82/9	83/9	84/9
1-2 P.M..............					85/9	86/9	87/9
2-3 P.M..............					88/9	89/9	90/9
3-4 P.M..............					91/9	92/9	93/9
4-5 P.M..............					94/9	95/9	96/9
5-6 P.M..............					97/9	98/9	99/9
6-7 P.M..............					100/9	101/9	102/9
7-8 P.M..............					103/9	104/9	105/9
8-9 P.M..............					106/9	107/9	108/9
9-10 P.M.............					109/9	110/9	111/9
10-11 P.M............					112/9	113/9	114/9
11-12 P.M............					115/9	116/9	117/9
12-1 A.M.............					118/9	119/9	120/9
1-2 A.M..............					121/9	122/9	123/9
2-3 A.M..............					124/9	125/9	126/9

14. Now I'd like to talk about the kinds of things you did yesterday evening, TV watching or anything else. I'm interested in the main things you did between seven and eleven, at home or at other places, and whom you were with.

Let's begin with the period 7:00 to 7:30.

(IF AT HOME)

	What doing? (If TV, what program or channel?)	Where? (i.e., out/at home)		With whom? (Relationship)	Anything else at same time?
		out	at home		
7:00-7:30..					
7:30-8:00..					
8:00-8:30..					
8:30-9:00..					
9:00-9:30..					
9:30-10:00.					
10:00-10:30					
10:30-11:00					

15. Television programs can be designed to provide different things. From your point of view, does television today have enough, not enough, or too many of each of these kinds of programs?

First, how about educational programs? Would you say there are enough, not enough, or too many educational programs?

    Enough.......... 1
    Not enough...... 2
    Too many........ 3
    Don't know...... 8   127/9

16a. How about educational programs intended mainly for children, would you say there are enough, not enough, or too many?

    Enough.......... 1⎤   128/9
    Not enough...... 2⎬(ASK b)
    Too many........ 3⎦
    Don't know...... 8 (SKIP TO 17a)

b. Can you give me an idea or an example of the kind of educational program for children you have in mind when you say that there are (enough, not enough, too many) of them? (RECORD VERBATIM)

    ☐☐ 129-130/9

17a. How about educational programs intended mainly for adults, would you say there are enough, not enough, or too many?

    Enough.......... 1⎤ 131/9
    Not enough...... 2⎬(ASK b)
    Too many........ 3⎦
    Don't know...... 8 (SKIP TO 18)

b. Can you give me an idea or an example of the kind of educational program for adults you have in mind when you say that there are (enough, not enough, too many) of them? (RECORD VERBATIM)

    ☐☐ 132-133/9

18. How about programs that provide escape from everyday life--does television today have enough, not enough, or too many programs of that type?

    Enough........ 1
    Not enough..... 2
    Too many....... 3
    Don't know..... 8   134/9

19a. How about programs that offer advice or help solve problems, would you say there are enough, not enough or too many?

    Enough........ 1⎤ 135/9
    Not enough..... 2⎬(ASK b)
    Too many....... 3⎦
    Don't know..... 8 (SKIP TO 20)

b. Can you give me an idea or example of the kind of advice program you have in mind? (RECORD VERBATIM)

    ☐☐ 136-137/9

20. And programs that provide just plain laughs. Are there enough, not enough, or too many?

    Enough........ 1
    Not enough..... 2
    Too many....... 3
    Don't know..... 8   138/9

21. Programs that provide information about politics and political candidates, are there enough, not enough or too many?

    Enough........ 1
    Not enough..... 2
    Too many....... 3
    Don't know..... 8   139/9

22. And programs that provide information about national problems in the U.S., like inflation and the energy shortage, are there enough, not enough or too many?

    Enough........ 1
    Not enough..... 2
    Too many....... 3
    Don't know..... 8   140/9

23. Now would you please tell me something about what you do to decide on which TV programs to watch? For example, do you often, occasionally, or practically never: (READ EACH PROPOSITION)

	Often	Occasionally	Practically never, Never	Don't know	
a. Make selections from TV Guide, or some other weekly listing of programs?........................	1	2	3	8	141/9
b. Watch the same shows because you like them and know when they are on?...........................	1	2	3	8	142/9
c. Follow recommendations of friends and relatives?...	1	2	3	8	143/9
d. Look up TV shows to watch several days in advance?.	1	2	3	8	144/9
e. Turn the dial until you find something interesting?	1	2	3	8	145/9
f. Read the listings that appear each day in the newspaper?..	1	2	3	8	146/9
g. Watch one program and then just leave the set turned to the same station?.......................	1	2	3	8	147/9
h. Follow recommendations given to your children by school teachers?..................................	1	2	3	8	148/9
i. Select from advertisements that appear on TV?......	1	2	3	8	149/9
j. Watch shows picked by other family members?........	1	2	3	8	150/9

24. What are some of your favorite programs--those you watch regularly or whenever you get a chance? (RECORD VERBATIM)

26. Do you think that you spend too much time watching television, or would you say that you don't have a chance to see as much as you would really like to?

    Spend too much time............. 1

    Don't have chance to see enough. 2

    Right amount.................... 3

    Other answer (VERBATIM) (write in)

    _____ 4

    _____

    Don't know..................... 8   154/9

27. Generally speaking, would you say that television should do more in the way of providing informational material, or should it concentrate on providing the best entertainment possible?

    Provide more informational
    material......................... 1

    Provide best entertainment........ 2

    Don't know, both, can't choose.... 8   155/9

25. Television programs, like most other things, vary in quality. Some are better than others. Considering just the programs you generally watch, what proportion would you say are extremely enjoyable, how many are somewhat enjoyable, how many are just so-so, and how many are disappointing? First, roughly, what percentage of the TV programs you watch would you call "extremely enjoyable"? (WHEREVER POSSIBLE, GET PERCENTAGE FOR EACH CATEGORY--IT'S OKAY IF THEY DON'T ADD UP TO 100%)

    Extremely enjoyable... _____ %

    Somewhat enjoyable.... _____ %

    So-so................. _____ %

    Disappointing......... _____ %   151-153/9

28. Here are some statements about commercials. I'd like you to read each statement and mark whether you generally agree or disagree with each statement. (HAND PAGE 11 TO RESPONDENT)

28. (QUICKLY CHECK ✓ ONE COLUMN FOR EACH OF THE FOLLOWING TO SHOW WHETHER YOU GENERALLY AGREE OR DISAGREE WITH THE STATEMENT)

	Agree	Disagree	
a. Most commercials are too long......			156/9
b. I frequently find myself welcoming a commercial break................			157/9
c. I'd rather pay a small amount yearly if I could, to have television without commercials.....			158/9
d. Some commercials are so good that they are more entertaining than the program........................			159/9
e. I find some commercials very helpful in keeping me informed.....			160/9
f. I would prefer TV without commercials........................			161/9
g. Commercials are ordinarily in poor taste and very annoying...........			162/9
h. Commercials are a fair "price" to pay for the entertainment you get..			163/9
i. There are just too many commercials			164/9

29a. Are there any products or kinds of things now advertised on TV that you think should <u>not</u> be advertised on television?

      Yes.......   1   (ASK b)

      No........   2 ⎤

                    ⎬(SKIP TO 30a)

      Don't know   8 ⎦   165/9

  b. What things are these?   (RECORD VERBATIM)

30a. Aside from the things advertised, is there anything that goes on in commercials that you object to?

      Yes.......   1   (ASK b)

      No........   2 ⎤

                    ⎬(SKIP TO 31)

      Don't know   8 ⎦   166/9

  b. What do you object to?   (RECORD VERBATIM)

31. There has been a lot of discussion about the possible effects of television on children. Taking everything into consideration, would you say that children are better off with television or better off without television?

         With..........   1   (ASK 32)

         Without.......   2   (SKIP TO 35)

         Don't know....   8   (SKIP TO 38)

                                167/9

32. What do you think are some of the main advantages of television for children? (RECORD VERBATIM)

33. And what are some of the disadvantages, if any? (RECORD VERBATIM)

34. Can you think of any actual example where some child you know or have heard about has benefited from television? (What program was it that helped?) (Just what happened? In what way did the child benefit?) (RECORD VERBATIM)

                                               (SKIP TO 38)

(IF CHILDREN BETTER OFF "WITHOUT," ASK 35-37)

35. What do you think are some of the main disadvantages of television for children? (RECORD VERBATIM)

36. And what might be some of the advantages, if any? (RECORD VERBATIM)

37a. Can you think of an actual example where some child you know or have heard of has been harmed or has done something harmful as a result of television?

```
         Yes..........  1  (ASK b)
         No...........  2 ⎤
                          ⎬(SKIP TO 38)
         Don't know....  8 ⎦            168/9
```

b. Just what happened? What harm resulted? (RECORD VERBATIM)

(UNLESS OBVIOUS FROM 37b, ASK:)
c. Did that incident involve a child that you or someone you know knows personally, or was this something that you heard about some other way such as radio, newspapers, or magazines?

```
   Respondent knows child.....  1

   Respondent heard about
   some other way.............  2

   Don't know.................  8
                                     169/9
```

38. Now, a few questions on the specific effects television might have in making some children act or behave differently from others:

For instance, who do you think are likely to do better in school--children who watch a lot of television, or children who watch very little, or do you think the amount of watching TV doesn't make much difference in how they do in school?

```
   Children watching a lot...................  1
   Children watching very little............  2
   Not much difference......................  3
   Depends (vol.)_____  4
                        (on what?)
   Don't know...............................  8
                                               170/9
```

39. Who do you think are more likely to get into trouble, children who watch a lot of television, or children who watch very little, or do you think the amount of television watching doesn't make much difference in whether or not they get into trouble?

```
   Watch TV a lot...........................  1
   Watch TV very little.....................  2
   Not much difference......................  3
   Depends (vol.)_____  4
                        (on what?)
   Don't know...............................  8
                                               171/9
```

40. And how about reading books, do you think children who watch television a lot are apt to read more books, or do those who watch very little read more books, or do you think the amount of television watching doesn't make much difference in their reading of books?

```
   Watch TV a lot...........................  1
   Watch TV very little.....................  2
   Not much difference......................  3
   Depends (vol.) _____  4
                        (on what?)
   Don't know...............................  8
                                               172/9
```

41. Who do you think are more likely to grow up with better health, children who watch TV a lot, or those who watch very little, or do you think the amount of TV they watch doesn't make much difference to their health?

```
   Watch TV a lot...........................  1
   Watch TV very little.....................  2
   Not much difference......................  3
   Depends (vol.) _____  4
                        (on what?)
   Don't know...............................  8
                                               173/9
```

42. Who do you think are more likely to be better informed about what is going on in the world, children who watch TV a lot, or those who watch very little, or do you think the amount of TV they watch doesn't make much difference in how well informed they are about the world?

Watch TV a lot......................... 1

Watch TV very little.................. 2

Not much difference................... 3

Depends (vol.)_____ 4
                    (on what?)

Don't know............................ 8

174/9

43. Who do you think are more likely to get along better with other people when they grow up, children who watch TV a lot, or those who watch very little, or do you think the amount of TV they watch doesn't make much difference?

Watch TV a lot......................... 1

Watch TV very little.................. 2

Not much difference................... 3

Depends (vol.)_____ 4
                    (on what?)

Don't know............................ 8

175/9

44a. Do you have any children under 15 years old living here now?

Yes.......... 1 (ASK b)

No.......... 2 ⎤
              ⎬(SKIP TO 51)
Don't know... 8 ⎦   176/9

b. INTERVIEWER: ASK IF RESPONDENT IS THE PARENT (WHICH INCLUDES STEP AND FOSTER PARENTS) AND RECORD BELOW:

Parent....... 1 (ASK 45)

Other........ 2 (SKIP TO 51)

177/9

45. First, I'd like to know how many children you have under 15?

_____
(Number of children)   178-179/9

46. GET AGE AND SEX OF EACH CHILD UNDER 15:

Age at last birthday					
Sex					

DIRECTION: IF NO CHILDREN BETWEEN 1 AND 15 YEARS OLD, SKIP TO 51.

(IF ANY CHILDREN BETWEEN 1 AND 15 YEARS OLD:)

47. Which of the programs your (child watches/ children watch) do you think are the best programs for (him/her/them)? (RECORD VERBATIM)

48. And which programs your (child watches/children watch) aren't you too happy about? (RECORD VERBATIM)

49. Even though they're not always enforced 100%, are there any rules or regulations in your home about when and what your (child/children) watch, or do you let (him/her/them) make their own decisions? (RECORD VERBATIM)

DIRECTION: ASK QUESTION 50a THROUGH g OF PARENTS FOR ONE CHILD 4 THROUGH 12 YEARS OLD. IF MORE THAN ONE IN
THAT AGE GROUP, ASK ABOUT ONE NEAREST TO 8 YEARS OLD. SEE QUESTION 46. IF TWO CHILDREN
EQUIDISTANT, ARBITRARILY PICK ONE AND WRITE IN: AGE AND SEX OF CHILD ASKING ABOUT
IF NO CHILDREN 4 THROUGH 12 YEARS OLD, SKIP TO 51.

	(Sex)	(Age)
	180/9	181-182/9

50. Here are some things parents have told us they do with their children about TV. (Taking just one of your
children) Do you or your (husband/wife) often, occasionally, or never (each proposition):

	Often	Occasionally	Never	Don't know	
a. Set special hours when (child) can watch TV?	1	2	3	8	183/9
b. Restrict the total amount of time (child) can watch?.....................................	1	2	3	8	184/9
c. Decide the program (child) can watch?........	1	2	3	8	185/9
d. Encourage (child) to watch to keep him (her) quiet or occupied?...........................	1	2	3	8	186/9
e. Encourage (child) to watch to keep him (her) at home?.....................................	1	2	3	8	187/9
f. Make (child) change the channel when you see him (her) watching something you don't approve of?...	1	2	3	8	188/9
g. Forbid (child) to watch certain programs altogether?...................................	1	2	3	8	189/9

51. Do you find that you yourself are now watching TV more, or less, or about the same as you were ten years
ago?

More..............	1	
Less..............	2	
Same..............	3	
Don't know........	8	190/9

52. Now, how about changes that have taken place in TV over the past ten years? What do you see as some of
the important changes that have taken place? (RECORD VERBATIM)

53a. Here are some ways people have noticed that TV has changed over the past ten years. (HAND RESPONDENT CARD)
Would you read down that list and for each one tell me whether that is a change you have noticed or not?

	53a.			53b.				
	Noticed	Not noticed	Don't know	Change for better	Change for worse	No differ-ence	Don't know	
a. More live sports programs especially in the evening	1	2	3	4	5	6	8	191/9
b. Women taking more important roles in entertainment programs.................	1	2	3	4	5	6	8	192/9
c. Reruns of old series from previous years...........	1	2	3	4	5	6	8	193/9
d. More time devoted to local news programs............	1	2	3	4	5	6	8	194/9
e. More substitution of specials for the regular programs.................	1	2	3	4	5	6	8	195/9
f. Greater variety of programs in the late evening--after 11 or so.................	1	2	3	4	5	6	8	196/9
g. Movies made especially for television...........	1	2	3	4	5	6	8	197/9
h. Mini-series programs in prime time..............	1	2	3	4	5	6	8	198/9
i. More open treatment of sex on TV.....................	1	2	3	4	5	6	8	199/9
j. More open treatment of problems like drugs and race relations...........	1	2	3	4	5	6	8	200/9
k. More light conversation among members of local news teams...............	1	2	3	4	5	6	8	201/9
l. The "advisories" or "warn-ings" that are sometimes given at the start of programs.................	1	2	3	4	5	6	8	202/9
m. More women presenting the news.....................	1	2	3	4	5	6	8	203/9
n. More programs with blacks in important roles........	1	2	3	4	5	6	8	204/9

53b. Now I'm going to repeat the changes you have noticed, and for each one would you tell me, as far as your own viewing is concerned, if this has been a change for the <u>better</u>, a change for the <u>worse</u>, or if it hasn't made any difference to you? (HAND RESPONDENT CARD) First, <u>(read letter of first item noticed)</u>. (ASK ABOUT EACH ONE NOTICED) (RECORD ABOVE)

---

54. Compared to 10 years ago, do you think that the way the news is presented on TV is generally better, or generally worse, or has it stayed about the same?

Better...... 1   Stayed the same 3

Worse....... 2   Don't know..... 8

205/9

55. How about the entertainment programs in evening prime time? As compared to 10 years ago, do you think they have gotten better, or worse, or stayed about the same?

Better...... 1   Stayed the same 3

Worse....... 2   Don't know..... 8

206/9

56a. Are there any kinds of programs you are watching more of now than you used to 10 years ago?

Yes........ 1 (ASK b)

No......... 2 (SKIP TO 57)   207/9

b. What kinds? (RECORD VERBATIM)

57. Can you think of the one biggest moment on TV for you--the time you would have missed TV the most if you couldn't have watched what was on?

Yes........... 1 (ASK 58)

No............ 2 ⎫

Don't know..... 8 ⎬ (SKIP TO 59)   208/9

58. When was that--what were you watching? (RECORD VERBATIM)

[| |] 209-211/9

59. In your opinion, how good a job has TV been doing in covering what is going on in Iran: excellent, good, only fair, or poor?

Excellent......... 1

Good.............. 2

Only fair......... 3

Poor.............. 4

Don't know........ 8   212/9

60. Up to now, how good a job has TV been doing in presenting the issues and candidates for the 1980 elections: excellent, good, only fair or poor?

Excellent......... 1

Good.............. 2

Only fair......... 3

Poor.............. 4

Don't know........ 8   213/9

61. Do you feel that TV plays a very important part, a fairly important part, or no part at all in helping you to decide whom to vote for in an election?

Very important.... 1

Fairly important.. 2

No part........... 3

Don't know........ 8   214/9

62a. Thinking of the people that give the news on TV, in general, do you feel that they let their own opinions color the way they give the news, or do they generally give the news straight, as it happened?

Color news.......... 1 (ASK b)

Straight............ 2 (SKIP TO 63)

Mixed: Some color, some don't.......... 3 (ASK b)

Don't know.......... 8 (SKIP TO 63)   215/9

b. How--in what way do you think they color it? (RECORD VERBATIM)

[|] 216-217/9

63. Is there any one newscaster you like to watch on TV more than others? (IF "YES") Who?

_____ (ASK 64a)
(WRITE IN NAME OF NEWSCASTER)   218-220/9

No one newscaster... 8 (SKIP TO 65)   221/9

64a. In the way __(newscaster in 63)__ presents the news, does he/she give the impression of being liberal, conservative, or middle-of-the-road, or can't you tell?

Liberal.............. 1

Conservative......... 2

Middle-of-the-road..... 3

Don't know, can't tell. 8   222/9

b. Do you feel that __(newscaster in 63)__ lets his own opinions color the way he/she gives the news, or does he/she generally give the news straight, as it happened?

Color news............ 1

Straight.............. 2

Mixed: some colored, some straight.......... 3

Don't know............ 8   223/9

65. The public television stations are the ones that have no commercial advertisements on them--such as channel _____ .

Are there any public broadcasting TV stations that you can receive in this home?

Yes .... 1 (ASK 66)
No............ 2
Don't know.... 8 } (SKIP TO 71)   224/9

66. Do you ever watch (this/any of these) stations)?

Yes........... 1 (ASK 67)
No............ 2
Don't know.... 8 } (SKIP TO 71)   225/9

67. About how often do you usually watch public television, once a week or more often, or less often than once a week?

Once a week or more often 1 (ASK 68)
Less often.............. 2
Don't know.............. 8 } (SKIP TO 69)   226/9

68. On the average, about how many hours a week do you watch public television?

_____   227-228/9
(Number of hours)

69. Do any other people living here watch public television once a week or more often?

Yes........... 1 (ASK 70)
No............ 2
Don't know.... 8 } (SKIP TO 71)   229/9

70. Who else in the household watches public television as often as once a week? (LIST RELATIONSHIP: DAUGHTER, WIFE, HOUSEMATE, ETC.)

71. Now I have a few more questions about cable TV. Just to be sure I have the right information, did you say you have cable? (CHECK ONE)

Have cable........ 1 (ASK 72)
Don't have cable... 2 (SKIP TO 74)   230/9

72. About how long have you had it?

Less than a year... 1
1-2 years.......... 2
3 years +.......... 3
Don't know........ 8   231/9

73. What was the main reason for getting it? (RECORD VERBATIM)

[|]   232-233/9

Now, just a few questions for tabulation purposes.

74. Are you now married, separated, divorced, widowed, or have you never been married?

Married......... 1

Separated....... 2

Divorced........ 3

Widowed......... 4

Never married... 5

Don't know...... 8   234/9

75. What was the last year of regular school that you completed--not counting specialized schools like secretarial, art or trade school? (IF RESPONDENT IS MARRIED, ASK:) And what was the last year of regular school your (husband,wife) completed?

Years completed:	Respondent	Spouse
0-4 years..............	1	1
5-6 years..............	2	2
7-8 years..............	3	3
9-11 years.............	4	4
12 years..............	5	5
1-2 years college.......	6	6
3-4 years college.......	7	7
Don't know.............	8	8

235-236/9

76a. Are you employed--either full or part time?

    Full time...... 1 ⎫
                  ⎬ (SKIP TO c)
    Part time...... 2 ⎭

    Not employed... 3 (ASK b)   237/9

b. Are you: (READ APPROPRIATE CATEGORIES)

    Housewife...... 1 ⎫
    Unemployed..... 2 ⎪
    Student........ 3 ⎬ (SKIP TO 77)
    Retired........ 4 ⎪
    Other.......... 5 ⎭   238/9

c. Exactly what sort of work do you do?

    Occupation_____

    Industry _____

    239-240/9

77. Are you the head of the household?

    Yes..... 1 (SKIP TO 79)

    No...... 2 (ASK 78a)   241/9

78a. Is (head of household) employed--either full or part time?

    Full time...... 1 ⎫
                  ⎬ (SKIP TO c)
    Part time...... 2 ⎭

    Not employed... 3 (ASK b)   242/9

b. Is (he/she): (READ APPROPRIATE CATEGORIES)

    Housewife...... 1 ⎫
    Unemployed..... 2 ⎪
    Student........ 3 ⎬ (SKIP TO 79)
    Retired........ 4 ⎪
    Other.......... 5 ⎭   243/9

c. Exactly what sort of work does (he/she) do?

    Occupation_____

    Industry _____

    244-245/9

79. What is your (approximate) age?

    _____ 246-247/9
       (age)

80. In which of these general groups did your total family income fall last year--before taxes, that is? (HAND RESPONDENT CARD)

    a. Under $3,000........ 00

    b. $ 3,000 - $ 6,999... 01

    c. $ 7,000 - $ 9,999... 02

    d. $10,000 - $14,999... 03

    e. $15,000 - $19,999... 04

    f. $20,000 - $24,999... 05

    g. $25,000 - $39,999... 06

    h. $40,000 and over.... 07

    Don't know......... 08   248/9

81. Regardless of how you have voted in the past, what do you usually consider yourself--a Democrat, a Republican, some other party, or what?

    Democrat............... 1

    Republican............. 2

    Other specific party... 3

    Independent (vol.)..... 4

    Don't know............. 8   249/9

82. Do you consider yourself a Conservative or a Liberal, or what?

    Conservative........... 1

    Liberal................ 2

    Middle-of-the-road (vol.) 3

    Other (write in)_____ 4

    Don't know............. 8   250/9

83. What is your religious preference (what do you consider yourself)?

    Protestant............. 1

    Catholic............... 2

    Jewish................. 3

    Other (write in)_____ 4

    Don't know............. 8   251/9

84a. Some time back we asked about children under 15, so we have that information. But now I'd just like to
know whether there are any young people living here who are 15 up to 20 years old (15, 16, 17, 18, or
19 years old).

Yes.......... 1 (ASK b)

No........... 2 (SKIP TO 85)   252/9

b. How old and what sex are they?   (GET AGE AND SEX OF EACH CHILD 15 UP TO 20 YEARS OLD)

Age at last birthday							
Sex							

TO BE COMPLETED BY INTERVIEWER

85. Race:

   White........ 1

   Black........ 2

   Other........ 3   253/9

86. Sex:

   Male......... 1

   Female....... 2   254/9

87. Respondent is:

WHITE { Designated respondent....... 1
FORM   { Other eligible.............. 2

BLUE { 28,29 year old oversample... 3
FORM { 38,39 year old oversample... 4   255/9

Name_____ _____

Address_____ _____ _____

City or town_____ State_____ Zip code_____

Apt. #_____

Tele.#_____ Area code _____

Date_____

Interviewer's initials _____

Statistical Notes

Confidence Limits and Statistical Significance

In the body of this report we have not presented confidence intervals for estimates based on the samples nor for differences between percentages found in the various tables. The establishment of such intervals is complicated by the fact that the data reported are derived from three sample surveys that used similar but not identical multistage area-probability procedures, all involving some clustering.

For rough estimates, somewhat on the conservative side, we are presenting two tables based on reasonable assumptions concerning the effects of sample stratification and clustering; more detailed tables can be found in many standard statistical texts. The first gives the confidence interval for the proportions of the three total samples in their answers to individual questions. For example, if 20 percent of 1900 respondents in the 1970 survey answered "yes" to a question, we could say with 95 percent confidence (i.e., we would expect the statement to be correct in 95 cases out of 100) that the percentage for the total population from which the sample was chosen would be between 17 and 23 percent (plus or minus 3 percent).

The second table shows the percentage differences required for statistical significance at the 5 percent level for different subsample sizes. For example, it would take a difference of about nine percentage points for a finding of significance between the answers of 200 teenagers and 2000 adults, when each group gave a response somewhere in the 35 to 65 percent range. For percentage differences in that range, for total samples (e.g., 1970 versus 1980), the requirement would be about 4 percentage points.

Multivariate Analyses

A computer program called Automatic Interaction Detection (AID) was employed at several points in our analysis of the 1960, 1970, and 1980 data. The program is designed to take into account the inter-

Table C.1 95% Confidence Intervals for Estimates

Proportion Near	1960 Sample	1970 Sample	1980 Sample
90	2	2	2
80	3	3	3
70	3	4	4
60	3	4	4
50	3	4	4
40	3	4	4
30	3	4	4
20	3	3	3
10	2	2	2

Table C.2 Differences Between Percentages Required for Significance

Number of Cases	Number of Cases						
	2000	1000	700	500	400	300	200
FOR PERCENTAGES FROM 35 TO 65							
2000	4	5	6	7	7	8	9
1000		6	6	7	8	8	10
700			7	8	8	9	10
500				8	9	9	10
400					9	10	11
300						10	11
200							12
FOR PERCENTAGES AROUND 20 AND 80							
2000	3	4	5	5	6	6	8
1000		5	5	6	6	7	8
700			6	6	6	7	8
500				7	7	7	9
400					7	8	9
300						8	9
200							10

relationships of several independent, or predictor, variables and indicate to extent to which each combination of them contributes to an explanation of one dependent, or criterion, variable (in our case attitude toward television, amount of viewing, and use of cable). The program proceeds by dichotomizing each predictor variable, selecting the one that serves as the best predictor. This split defines two groups, each of which is separately subjected to the same dichotomization procedure. The process continues until no further differences can be found at a prespecified level of significance. For a full description of the technique, see John A. Sonquist, Multivariate Model Building, Ann Arbor: Institute of Social Research, 1970.

References

Adler, Richard, ed. 1981. *Understanding Television: Essays on Television as a Social and Cultural Force.* New York: Praeger.

Barton, Judith S., ed. 1984. *Guide to the Bureau of Applied Social Research,* New York: Clearwater.

Bartos, Rena and Theodore E. Dunn. 1976. *Advertising and Consumers.* New York: American Association of Advertising Agencies.

Berelson, Bernard. 1949. "Progress in Communictions Research: What 'Missing the Newspaper' Means." In Paul F. Lazarsfeld and Frank N. Stanton, eds. *Communications Research.* New York: Harper.

—— 1952. *Content Analysis in Communication Research.* Glencoe, Ill.: Free Press.

Blumler, Jay G. and Elihu Katz, eds. 1974. *The Uses of Mass Communications: Current Perspectives on Gratifications Research.* Sage Annual Reviews of Communication Research, vol. 3. Beverly Hills: Sage.

Blumler, Jay G. and Denis McQuail, eds. 1969. *Television in Politics.* Chicago: University of Chicago Press.

Bogart, Leo 1956. *The Age of Television: A Study of Viewing Habits and the Impact of Television on American Life.* New York: Ungar.

—— 1965. "The Mass Media and the Blue Collar Worker." In A. Shostak and W. Gomberg, eds. *Blue Collar World: Studies of the American Worker.* Englewood Cliffs, N.J.: Prentice-Hall.

Bower, Robert T. 1973. *Television and the Public.* New York: Holt, Rinehart and Winston.

Bybee, Carl., Joseph Turow, and James D. Robinson. 1982. "Mass Media Scholars' Belief About the Impact of Television on Children." Paper presented at the 37th Annual Meeting of the American Association for Public Opinion Research, Baltimore, May 20–23.

Campbell, Angus. 1966. "Has Television Reshaped Politics?" In E. C. Dreyer and W. A. Rosenbaum, eds. *Political Opinion and Electoral Behavior.* Belmont, Calif.: Wadsworth.

Chu, Goodwin C. and Wilbur Schramm. 1968. *Learning from Television: What the Research Says.* Washington, D.C.: National Association of Educational Broadcasters.

—— 1975. *Learning from Television.* Washington, D.C.: National Society of Professionals in Telecommunications.

Comstock, George A, Steven Chaffee, Natan Katzman, Maxwell McCombs and Donald Roberts. 1978. *Television and Human Behavior.* New York: Columbia University Press.

Comstock, George A, Eli A. Rubenstein and John P. Murray, eds. 1972. *Television and Social Behavior: A Technical Report to the Surgeon General's Scientific Advisory Committee on Television and Social Behavior.* Rockville, Md.: U.S. Department of HEW.

Council for Basic Education, 1982. *Basic Education.* Washington, D.C., vol 27, no. 4.

Cutler, Neal. 1969 "Generation Maturity and Party Affiliation." *Public Opinion Quarterly* (Winter), pp. 583–589.

Davison, W. Phillips and Frederick T. C. Yu, eds. 1974. *Mass Communication Research: Major Issues and Future Directions.* New York: Praeger.

Efron, Edith. 1971. *The News Twisters.* Los Angeles: Nash Publishing.

Feschbach, S. 1971. "Reality and Fantasy in Filmed Violence." In J. P. Murray et al., eds. *Television and Social Behavior.* Vol. 2. *Television and Social Learning.* Rockville, Md.: U.S. National Institute of Mental Health.

Frank, Ronald E. and Marshall G. Greenberg. 1980. *The Public's Use of Television.* Beverly Hills: Sage.

Gerbner, G., L. Gross, M. F. Eleey, M. Jackson-Beeck, S. Jeffries-Fox and N. Signorielli. 1977. *Violence Profile No. 8: Trends in Network Television Drama and Viewer Conceptions of Social Reality, 1967–1976.* Philadelphia: Annenberg School of Communications.

Gerson, W. M. 1966. "Mass Media Socialization Behavior: Negro-White Differences." *Social Forces* 45:40–50.

Glaser, William. 1965. "Television and Voter Turnout." *Public Opinion Quarterly* (Spring), pp. 71–87.

Greenberg, Bradley S. and Brenda Dervin. 1971. *Use of Mass Communication by the Urban Poor.* New York: Praeger.

Hart, Peter, 1979. *A Survey of Attitudes Toward Public Television.* Washington, D.C.: Peter Hart Research Association.

Herzog, Herta. 1944. "What Do We Really Know About Daytime Serial Listeners?" In Paul J. Lazersfeld and Frank N. Stanton, eds. *Radio Research 1942–1943.* New York: Duell, Sloan and Pearce.

Himmelweit, Hilde T., A. N. Oppenheimer and Pamela Vince. 1958. *Television and the Child.* London: Oxford University Press.

Jacobson, Harvey. 1969. "Mass Media Believability: A Study of Receiver Judgments." *Journalism Quarterly* (Spring), pp. 20–28.

Katz, Elihu, Michael Gurvitch and Hadassah Haas. 1973. "On the Use of Mass Media for Important Things." *American Sociological Review,* vol. 38, no. 2

Katz, Elihu and Paul F. Lazarsfeld. 1955. *Personal Influence: The Part Played by People in the Flow of Mass Communications.* Glencoe, Ill.: Free Press.

Katzman, Nathan. 1975. *Public Television Programming by Category, Fiscal Year 1974.* Washington, D.C.: Corporation for Public Broadcasting.

Katzman, Solomon and Nathan Katzman. 1982. *Public Television Programming by Category, Fiscal Year 1980.* Washington, D.C.: Corporation for Public Broadcasting.

Klapper, Joseph. 1960. *The Effects of Mass Communication.* Glencoe, Ill.: Free Press.

Lang, Kurt and Gladys Engel Lang. 1968. *Politics and Television.* New York: Quadrangle.

Lazarsfeld, Paul F. 1940. *Radio and the Printed Page: An Introduction to the Study of Radio and Its Role in the Communication of Ideas.* New York: Duell, Sloan and Pearce.

Lazarsfeld, Paul F., Bernard Berelson and Hazel Gaudet. 1968. *The People's Choice: How the Voter Makes Up His Mind in a Presidential Campaign.* 3d ed. New York: Columbia University Press.

Lazarsfeld, Paul F. and Marjorie Fiske. 1938. "The Panel as a New Tool for Measuring Opinion." *Public Opinion Quarterly* (October), pp. 596–612.

Lazarsfeld, Paul F. and Frank N. Stanton, eds. 1941. *Radio Research 1941.* New York: Duell, Sloan and Pearce.

—— 1944. *Radio Research 1942–43.* New York: Duell, Sloan and Pearce.

—— *Communication Research 1948–1949.* New York: Harper.

Lyle, J. 1975. *The People Look at Public Television 1974.* Washington, D.C.: Corporation for Public Broadcasting.

McCombs, M. E. 1968. "Negro Use of Television and Newspapers for Political Information, 1952–1964." *Journal of Broadcasting* 12:261–266.

McCombs, M. E. and D. L. Shaw. 1972. "The Agenda-Setting Function of the Mass Media." *Public Opinion Quarterly* 36:176–187.

Mendelsohn, Harold and Irving Crespi. 1970. *Polls, Television and the New Politics.* Scranton, Pa.: Chandler.

Merton, Robert K. and Patricia Kendall. 1946. "The Focused Interview." *American Journal of Sociology* 51:541–557.

National Institute of Mental Health. 1971. *Television and Growing Up: The Impact of Television Violence.* Washington, D.C.

—— 1982. *Television and Behavior. Volume 1. Summary Report.* Washington, D.C.

NCPP *Newsletter,* 1972. Washington, D.C., vol. 1, no. 3. Report of the National Council on Public Polls.

Osgood, Charles E. 1967. *The Measurement of Meaning.* Urbana: University of Illinois Press.

Patterson, Thomas E. 1980. *The Mass Media Election: How Americans Choose Their President.* New York: Praeger.

Pool, Ithiel de Sola. 1983. *Technologies of Freedom.* Cambridge: Harvard University Press.

Robinson, John P. 1977. *How Americans Used Their Time in 1965.* New York: Praeger.

The Roper Organization. 1979. *Roper Reports,* No. 6.

The Roper Organization. 1981. *Roper Reports,* No. 5.

Roper Organization. 1981. *Cross Section Survey in April-May 1981.* New York.

—— 1983. *Trends in Attitudes Toward Television and Other Media: A 24-Year Review.* New York: Television Information Office.

Schramm, Wilbur, Jack Lyle, and Ithiel de Sola Pool. 1963. *The People Look at Educational Television.* Stanford: Stanford University Press.

Schramm, Wilbur, Jack Lyle, and Edwin B. Parker. 1961. *Television in the Lives of Our Children.* Stanford: Stanford University Press.

"Stations and Channels Receivable per TV Household." 1982. In *Nielsen Television Index.* New York: A. C. Nielsen.

Steiner, Gary A. 1963. *The People Look at Television.* New York: Knopf.

Sterling, Christopher H. 1980. *Broadcasting and Mass Communication: A Survey Bibliography.* 8th ed. Philadelphia: Temple University Department of Radio-TV-Film.

Stevenson, Robert L., Richard A. Eisenger, Barry M. Feinberg, and Alan B. Kotok. 1973. "Untwisting the News Twisters: A Replication of Efron's Study." *Journalism Quarterly* (Summer) 50:211–219.

Weaver, Paul H. 1972. "Is Television News Biased?" *Public Interest* (Winter) 26:57–74.

Weaver, Paul H., D. A. Graber, M. E. McCombs, and C. H. Eyal. 1981. *Media Agenda: Setting in a Presidential Election.* New York: Praeger.

Index